Voices of a Dream

Stories from

A Touch of Understanding®

Voices of a Dream

Published by A Touch of Understanding®Inc.
www.TouchOfUnderstanding.org

ISBN-10: 0-692-64590-X
ISBN-13: 978-0-692-64590-1
Library of Congress Control Number: 2016935945
Printed in the United States of America

Cover design and book layout, EditPros LLC

CATALOGING INFORMATION:

A Touch of Understanding

Visions of a Dream: Stories from A Touch of Understanding®

Filing categories:

BIO033000   BIOGRAPHY & AUTOBIOGRAPHY / People
with Disabilities

SOC029000   SOCIAL SCIENCE / People with Disabilities

OCC019000   BODY, MIND & SPIRIT / Inspiration &
Personal Growth

SEL031000   SELF-HELP / Personal Growth / General

Prologue

A Touch of Understanding® (ATOU) is a 501 (c) (3) non-profit organization started by Leslie DeDora and her father, Edward Ennis, in the early 1990s, in Granite Bay, California. The mission of A Touch of Understanding is to encourage acceptance and respect for all individuals. Its educational programs are designed to enhance understanding of differences, thereby minimizing discrimination, social isolation and bullying suffered by children and adults who are perceived as different for any reason, but especially those with disabilities.

Over the years, more than two hundred individuals have donated their time, energy, and expertise to ATOU. You will see by the multiple roles many people have played that ATOU team members are committed to our mission and to one another. Other than those in the Past and Present Staff Members Section, all contributors of stories for this book are volunteers.

Members of ATOU manage their challenges in ways that make their lives more personally enjoyable. In some cases, writing their stories was difficult because putting their honest thoughts and experiences onto paper made the stories more real. Although the editors had to shorten some of the stories and did some minor editing of grammar and spelling, they worked hard to maintain the authentic voices of the authors in their own words. We at ATOU hope that people will read all of these wonderful stories and gain admiration and appreciation for the resilience of the human spirit. We also hope readers will see how amazing ATOU is for bringing together a group of complete strangers to encourage acceptance and respect from all, and for all. This book is a tribute to ATOU and the incredible folks the organization has attracted with different stories, but similar goals to live happily. Read with an open mind and heart—and above all, enjoy! For more information, please visit the ATOU website: www.touchofunderstanding.org.

ATOU Co-Founder & Executive Director: Leslie DeDora

ATOU Co-Founder: Edward Ennis

Book Editors: Jill C. Mason and Bob Schultz

To my dear friend Laurie, Our childhood and friendship experiences are treasures to me and were inspiration for this program. With love and thanks, always, Les

The Vision

"It is in identifying yourself with the hopes, dreams, fears and longings of others that you may understand them and help them."
—Wilferd A. Peterson

Leslie DeDora

ATOU Co-Founder and Executive Director

Have you ever had a dream that made your heart beat faster every time you thought about it? That is what A Touch of Understanding was, and still is, to me. When ATOU was just a dream, every inspirational quote, sermon, or song I heard, every book I read made my heart beat faster. They all seemed to encourage me to pursue the dream of helping children understand the challenges of disabilities. It became something I could not NOT do and still be true to myself. I knew that if children, whose hearts are open to new ideas, could understand the disabling challenges, those challenges would no longer be barriers to friendship and acceptance. I envisioned children in wheelchairs, children with artificial limbs, children whose behavior or appearance isolated them, being included with all children, playing, learning, and

5

just being together. At that time, I could only imagine the lives ATOU would touch.

When I look back on the reasons for my passion for this mission, I realize they started when I was very young. The pieces all seem to fit together like interlocking building blocks. I viv-

Leslie and her Aunt Betty

idly remember being a five-year-old girl who inadvertently made my aunt cry. Aunt Betty had developmental and intellectual disabilities, known at the time as "mental retardation." In my eyes as a child, she appeared like the other adults, but be-

haved more like a child. I was confused and therefore behaved inappropriately. My mother learned of the incident and decided it was time to tell me, in terms a child could understand, about the challenges Aunt Betty faced. Because of her explanation, I began to understand and respect different abilities. This made it easy to befriend my peers with disabilities at school.

I had many friends with disabilities in elementary school. They were excluded from recess activities due to the rule that anyone with a disability or injury had to spend every recess in the principal's office. Since I was a very active kid and often injured myself, I spent many hours in the office with these children. We became good friends and remain so to this day.

The forced exclusion during recess made it very difficult for these kids to fit in during other school activities and for the other

6

students to get to know and befriend them. The disabilities were never explained to us and, as children will do, many filled in the blanks with misinformation and fear.

When we were in middle school and the hormones began to rage, the exclusion and isolation these kids faced in elementary school turned into torment. My heart still aches when I think of the things my friends heard people saying about them and the abuse they endured.

Fast forward twelve years: I became the mother of a young son, Paul. When he was three years old, I brought him to a junior museum. They had a display about disabilities. As I think back, it was a very sad display. It had an old wooden wheelchair, a pair of wooden crutches and, of all things, a coffin. I allowed Paul to sit in the wheelchair and handle the crutches. I didn't let him get into the coffin. Even as a three-year-old, he spoke of that experience for months. "Why would someone need wheels on their chair?" "Why do they need crutches?" "Will I need these someday?" It was clear that the hands-on opportunity anchored the experience in his young mind.

When Paul and my second son, Jason, were in elementary school, I volunteered in their classrooms. This was a time when schools were focused on mainstreaming students with special needs into the regular classrooms, rather than segregating them. I was excited to see this change, since I knew first-hand the damage of isolating children. However, I was saddened to see that these children with disabilities were often the object of teasing and bullying by their typically developing peers: A boy grabbed the crutches from a child who only had one leg, just as the recess bell rang; students sang in unison, "Don't ask him! He's STUPID!" when a child with learning disabilities was asked to answer a question; a boy stole a walker from a child with cerebral palsy as he walked to school. I realized these children were behaving this way for the same reason I mistreated my Aunt Betty.

These children didn't have the information needed to understand the challenges faced by their classmates. The situation wasn't fair to anyone. It certainly was not fair to the children with disabilities who were the victims. And it wasn't fair to the typically developing children, who were not given the information they needed and deserved to behave properly and be comfortable befriending the kids with disabilities.

While my sons were still in elementary school, I had the blessing of working as an instructional aide in a second grade classroom taught by a phenomenal teacher—Annmarie Mallo*. When I told her about my dream, she smiled and said, "So start it in our classroom!" We did just that, and other teachers in second grade requested their students' participation. Then, while on the sidelines of my son's soccer game, I told another mother about the program. She mentioned that she was the administrator of a private school and would like her students to participate. She contacted our local newspaper, *The Sacramento Bee*, and I began getting calls from individuals with disabilities who wanted to be involved. The program began to grow.

Dreams take time and prayer. Dreams take commitment and dedication. Dreams take others who see the vision and offer their support. My husband and sons, my parents, my brother and, in fact, my whole family embraced the vision. My father, Edward Ennis, who had recently retired, made ATOU his retirement career. Without his partnership, I cannot imagine ATOU existing. My friends, who are more like family, joined in and helped. They continue to support ATOU in countless ways.

*Annmarie Mallo, see page 16

Interlocking building blocks—life experiences linked together to create a dream, a mission, a passion: my dear Aunt Betty and the loving relationship we shared; my childhood experiences seeing my friends tormented; my children's experiences with their peers; and our experience at the junior museum showing the value of hands-on opportunities. These all came together to create the program we have now: in which children, young people, and adults gain information and insight into the challenges of others.

The two-part program allows for the benefit of hands-on stations as well as the opportunity to meet our volunteers who have disabilities. Students use wheelchairs, white canes and Braille equipment, handle braces and artificial limbs, and do exercises to understand invisible disabilities, such as learning disabilities and autism. Our volunteers who have disabilities share their experiences and insight with the students. These parts come together to break down the walls of misunderstanding and fear, and build bridges of acceptance, respect, and friendship. One of the most touching comments I've heard over the years came from Hope, an eleven-year-old girl with cerebral palsy, who uses two wooden walking sticks. Following our workshop she said, "After A Touch of Understanding, I no longer feel invisible! Kids come up to me and give me high fives and call me by name." She embodied my vision of children being together.

As I look back on the early years and my anticipation of what ATOU might become, I realize that one person's dream may be small, but with the help and support of others, truly miraculous things can happen. You will hear many of these voices in this book. I will be forever grateful to each and every one.

❦

"Train a child in the way he should go, and when he is old he will not turn from it."

—Proverbs 22:6

Edward Ennis

ATOU Co-Founder

ATOU gave me a chance to join my wonderful daughter, Leslie, in improving the lives of schoolchildren, their teachers, and their families.

I like to think that I may have helped contribute to the success of the organization. We blended Leslie's background in

Ed Ennis

education and my background in business into something more than a mere structure for the organization. Although it is not connected to any established religion, there's something spiritual about it. It has a mission.

The mission of ATOU is respect for oneself and for the rights and feelings of others. It favors respect over tolerance, believing respect to be a more positive and outreaching attitude. ATOU promotes fellowship and a feeling of welcome to all individuals, thereby reducing the chance of children feeling isolated and becoming loners.

Through generations, many children have been instructed by parents and guardians to look away when encountering a person with disabilities. How unfortunate for all parties. Eventually, "Don't stare" may lead to "Don't care." It is ATOU's vision to bring up a new generation of children who break the mold, an inclusive generation whose curiosity about disabilities is satisfied, in which

- fear of the unknown is erased;
- respect and friendship are offered;
- social circles are expanded;
- educational and career opportunities are extended; and
- corporate and economic levels are more accessible.

So much of ATOU's growth and success can be attributed to the people Leslie has attracted to it. It's rewarding for ATOU's volunteers, both with and without disabilities, who make the workshops possible, to see the transformation they inspire in children and adults. The disability-awareness workshop helps to break the barriers of discomfort and the unknown. The disability evaporates because it is overcome by the volunteer's personality.

It is heartwarming to see former students return as adults and tell about how they were transformed years before, when they went through the ATOU workshop. Leslie has encountered them in her travels. We also have those who went through the program as children coming back to volunteer as adults.

I was born in 1926. I grew up at a time that was far removed from understanding disabilities. ATOU is especially effective with somebody from my generation, to see children educated to welcome not only other children, but also adults with disabilities.

ATOU provided a purpose in my life that I wouldn't have had otherwise. Its development was very timely, since I was just retiring. It gave me something to look forward to everyday, a new purpose to educate and help direct the attitudes of children. It was rewarding to see the "Ah Ha" moments and children's eyes light up with new understanding. It was the ideal job. To hear from principals, teachers and parents of children's new understanding and behavior, made the early morning reveille worthwhile. Best of all, it is the opportunity to work with my wonderful daughter in launching and nurturing such a humane service as ATOU.

The Pioneers

"I know of no more encouraging fact than the unquestionable ability of man to elevate his life by a conscious endeavor."
—Henry David Thoreau

Jeanne Culhane

ATOU Workshop Activity Instructor and Graphic Artist

When my older brother Rob was about eight or nine years old, he started getting a rash all over his face and body. It was later diagnosed as Darier's Disease, which is an incurable genetic skin disorder. I know that people can be insensitive now, but in the 1960s, they were even more so. Once, we were standing in the check-out line at the grocery store and someone behind us came right up to him and said, "Ew, what's wrong with your skin? Can't you do something about that?" Rob ended up dropping out of high school because he was teased so much.

In 1997, I started volunteering at A Touch of Understanding. At that time I thought, "I don't know anyone who's disabled, but it's a good cause." We went to schools and gave kids an opportunity to have hands-on experience with tools that people

13

Jeanne Culhane

who are disabled use. They picked up prosthetics, used wheelchairs, and wrote their names in Braille. They also listened to speakers who have disabilities and got to ask them questions. When people are afraid of something, the natural response is to either shy away from it or make fun of it, and ATOU's goal is to take away the fear of the unknown. And this doesn't have to apply only to disabilities. All children want to fit in, and when they're just a little bit different—they could be taller or shorter or fatter or have funny hair—other kids might be afraid to ask, or just don't like the kids with differences. And then the kids who are different don't have friends. If they're not teased, they become invisible, which is almost as bad as being teased because when people don't see you, you feel like you don't exist. So ATOU is really about changing attitudes, about accepting people who are different.

Suddenly, I made the connection that this was important to me because of the experience in my own family. I didn't think of my brother as having had a disability, but then I realized that looking different can be as much of a "disability" as being physically unable to do things.

I wish that I could sit down with him now and talk about it. But I can't. He died in 1985, after taking his own life at the age of 43. An organization like A Touch of Understanding might have helped people be a little kinder to him. It might have made it easier for him to share what he was going through so that he wouldn't have felt so alone. Now we often come across kids with learning disabilities. We've actually had kids begin to cry when they do the mirror writing, or the experiencing the autism station and they hear others say, "This is really hard!" It's validation. There have been kids who have written letters to us afterwards saying, "I really appreciate (a certain person) now because I didn't realize how difficult it was for her/him to do something." We love that! That's when we know we're making a difference. We see ourselves as reflections in other people's eyes. A Touch of Understanding is about being aware of other people's feelings and seeing them for the beautiful people they are on the inside.

"Keep your face to the sunshine and you cannot see a shadow."
—Helen Keller

Terri Hollister

ATOU Volunteer

It is with great honor and pleasure that I write about my experience over the years with A Touch of Understanding. I was a second grade teacher at Greenhills Elementary School in Granite Bay, California, when Leslie DeDora, who was an instructional assistant, began her program with our second grade students. The students were in awe of Mrs. DeDora's stories of compassion and her wealth of knowledge. As a teacher, I was also very impressed with the way in which Mrs. DeDora shared her program and her message of empathy.

Terri Hollister

A few years later, I moved to another school and was visited by ATOU. The big difference (from when I first saw the

15

program) was the incredible group of speakers, the vast array of loving and patient volunteers, and the pride of the entire organization. Students and parents began chatting about the presentation and what they had learned. Students opened up about family members and their friends who may not have understood what is was like to live with a disability. My entire classroom culture was affected with a common cause of acceptance. I took pride in building a classroom culture built on trust, respect, and encouragement, and ATOU definitely paralleled with my beliefs.

Through the years, I have been amazed at ATOU's growth and development. I have attended workshops, trained as a volunteer, and have met the most kind and wise people who I can now call my friends. This organization has branched out to high schools, fundraisers, and art auctions. ATOU brings a wealth of opportunities for people of all ages to feel safe and respected. I am proud to be a member of ATOU!

"It takes little talent to see clearly what lies under one's nose, a good deal of it to know in which way to point that organ."

—*Wystan Hugh Auden*

Annmarie Mallo

Founding Board Vice President

Leslie DeDora had this unique idea that had been simmering and brewing for years in her heart and mind and, as it so happened, our paths crossed on a soccer field, well, more specifically, on the sidelines, during our sons' practice time. I was newly hired by the Eureka District to teach second grade at Greenhills School, while Leslie had just resigned from the district as a second grade classroom aide. After several sideline discussions (perhaps it was more like me begging, then asking the school principal,

Clara Taylor), Leslie graciously accepted my request to come back to Greenhills as my classroom aide (lucky me, in so many ways). Leslie was wonderful in every aspect of the classroom and so incredibly effective with our students in manner and instruction that I always said she made my job easy. I think we made a great duo and had a tremendous amount of fun working together.

Annmarie Mallo

Leslie and I talked often, and we had been working on her dream of a hands-on disability-awareness program for children. She had named it "Walk a Mile," which went along with the song "Walk a Mile in My Shoes," whose lyrics were in sync with what she wanted to convey (eventually the name changed to A Touch of Understanding with a logo of a hand, drawn by her son Jason). This program's purpose would be to demystify devices/tools that some people need to operate in this world, share the idea that some disabilities are hidden and, most importantly, demonstrate how on the inside, we humans are more alike than different.

At one point, we were discussing her ideas and I simply said, "Well, why don't you do it in here" (our classroom). That is all Leslie needed to hear to set her program in motion. She set up the first instruction in a format that used all the key components of a complete lesson, with the hands-on part being the center of it. Leslie had collected prosthetic devices, canes, and a wheelchair for the children to explore. She also discussed disabilities and abilities that we each might have, visible and invisible. I recall the students being fascinated and I, in turn, was awed by the depth of understanding the eight-year-olds gleaned from this first experience. For that first lesson, students could choose to use a wheelchair for a school day or part of a day for the experience of it. We found that first lesson to be quite impactful, but not necessarily feasible within our class and school time frame.

Also, in that first lesson, blindfolded students could tap through an obstacle course, simulating how a person without sight might navigate. As time progressed, other modifications came along, with more hands-on activities incorporated and wonderful volunteer speakers, who guided students through their world. The presentations, from the beginning started with Leslie telling about her Aunt Betty and the knitted blanket. The message from her dream never wavered.

Leslie encouraged students that first day, to say "Hello" the next time they encountered someone who used a wheelchair. The students and I came back in the next few weeks excited that we had done so. More importantly, we knew that person was like us in more ways than not. It was like a door opening for us all. From the first lesson in my classroom, the message was loud and clear and well-heard.

The program quickly grew at our school, as other second grade teachers started asking Leslie if she would offer the lesson to their classes. It wasn't long until other grade levels and district schools began requesting it.

The program's impact was tangible in our classroom and others. Children would reference the experience and use their newly acquired learning on the playground and with other students, recognizing differences with more acceptance. At class meetings, students' comments were direct results of having experienced the awareness the program encouraged. Students from the special day class, consisting of many children with disabilities, would be in our classroom for part of each day and, over the years, we experienced some very touching interactions.

One year, we had a couple of months to prepare for a non-verbal child with multiple issues stemming from a rare chromosome defect. During class meetings, we discussed how we might prepare for and help her in class and on the playground and what accommodations we could make to assist her, such as accompanying her to and from her other classroom, or how she might be included on the playground. Students were amazingly caring and concerned for her welfare the remainder of the year, and she became a natural part of the class. At our last class meeting, one of our brightest students complimented this student with severe disabilities for "teaching us" when he said, "We thought we were going to be the ones helping her." Simply said, and a very wise observation from an eight-year-old.

The years passed. The program expanded at an ever faster pace. From the first ATOU Board of Directors Leslie set up, which included her dad and mostly teachers and aides, the growth never stopped. An immense task and road lay ahead, but Leslie and the program remained steadfast in mission and determination. New board members added needed skills, fundraising ensued, and the numbers of students experiencing the program increased. The word started spreading, and the dream grew to what you see today.

So, my claim to fame with ATOU is being the "place" the dream, Leslie's vision, had the chance to unfold. All these years later with all that she has accomplished, busier than ever imaginable in the beginning, Leslie continually takes time to remind me and thank me for my small part in her dream.

*Annmarie is the teacher who helped to turn the ATOU dream into a reality. She is retired from the Eureka Union School District.

"That man is the richest whose pleasures are the cheapest."
—Henry David Thoreau

Paul Mitchell

ATOU Speaker

Paul Mitchell

I am a survivor of a serious auto accident that resulted in a traumatic brain injury. I use many compensatory strategies to minimize the negative effects. I live in Rocklin, California, I'm an artist, and I enjoy reading and watching movies. I am very social and thoroughly enjoy sharing my story with the students in A Touch of Understanding. I value being a presenter, because it allows me to grow as a person and helps others to better understand individuals who have more challenges than their own.

As I think about how A Touch of Understanding has impacted my life, I realize that it has changed me into a more complete person. How? By sharing my story with students, I hope that they gain insight into my experiences, and that my life can make a difference in theirs.

When I participate with the other volunteers, I gain inspiration, encouragement, and feel proud of our efforts. I realize that we are filling a specific need, and we receive consistent feedback that we touch a special chord in our listeners. If we can encourage mutual understanding and respect, we can change lives...including our own.

❧

"In the effort to give good and comforting answers to the young questioners who we love, we very often arrive at good and comforting answers for ourselves."

—*Ruth Goode*

Darlene O'Brien

ATOU Speaker, Trainer of ATOU Speakers, Volunteer Coordinator and Member of the ATOU Board of Directors

It was around 8 a.m. and the room was buzzing with activity as the ATOU crew hustled around, setting up their stations and getting things situated before the first group of students piled in. I found myself in the multipurpose room of a local elementary school in Roseville with the intention of observing a disability awareness and character-building workshop, which had recently been recommended to me by a friend. Not long after entering the room, I was warmly greeted by a woman introducing herself as Leslie DeDora. Other than a short phone call about a week earlier, this was our first meeting.

"Darlene?" Leslie began, "It's really nice to meet you. Thank you for coming to see what we do." Leslie then proceeded to introduce me to her father, and co-founder, Ed Ennis, and a few other volunteers, who were still whizzing by with things in their arms.

I found myself at ease. I remember one of my earliest impressions of that moment was being made to feel welcome and appreciated. I wasn't there to do anything meaningful, but still, Leslie and the others made me feel as though I belonged. What Leslie and the others did not know at the time of our first meeting, however, was how extraordinary it was for me to have been there in the first place. When I had agreed to come during that initial conversation with Leslie on the phone, I had not expressed to

Darlene O'Brien

her how branching out on my own to come and observe her workshop was a stretch for me in many ways.

I had only lost my sight twenty-one months earlier, and I was still doing my level best to adjust to my new state of being. Accepting invitations to visit school workshops on my own had not yet been in my repertoire. The fact that I was standing there with just my white cane and my nerve was big enough, but that was nothing compared to what happened next.

Not ten minutes after she had introduced herself to me, Leslie came back over and asked what turned out to be a profoundly life-altering question.

"Um, Darlene, I know you're only here today to observe, but we have a bit of a problem. We originally had two speakers scheduled to talk to the students today, but unfortunately one of those speakers just called to say he wasn't going to make it. I know this is short notice and everything, and I'm really sorry to ask you this, but would you be willing to take his place? We're scheduled to begin the workshop in five minutes, so there really isn't any time to call in someone else."

I was beyond shocked, and found myself speechless for a moment. Me be one of the speakers? But I didn't even know what it was they talked about. How was I supposed to just "fill-in"? I was afraid of screwing it up. After all, this was a well-established and polished gig already. What if I didn't live up to the expectations, whatever those expectations might be, considering I hadn't even seen the workshop yet? Man alive, I panicked as these thoughts ran through my mind. I asked Leslie what I would talk about, and she said to talk about myself, to tell the kids about my blindness and how I live my life as a person with no sight.

That sounded simple enough, right? Unfortunately for me, at that point in my life, I wasn't really sure how I was living with no sight. I really didn't have that part figured out yet. Every day of the past twenty-one months was spent trying to answer that question for myself, and I just didn't know if I could put that into words for the fourth graders I was being asked to speak to.

Well, of course I said yes, I would do it. Truthfully, in that moment, I could not have done anything else. I don't mean out of obligation or anything as cliché. No, it was deeper than that. As I stood there pondering what I could possibly say to the kids, it occurred to me that the only direction for me to go was forward. No matter what that looked like; forward meant saying "yes" to whatever presented itself to me. As I fondly look back on that moment, it truly proved to be a milestone in my life.

So off to the classroom we went. The other speaker took the lead and spoke first to the group of forty or so fourth graders. The kids listened with great attention and when the speaker was finished with his twenty-minute talk, they asked fantastic questions. Then, it was my turn.

I took a deep breath and introduced myself to the kids. After receiving a chorus of greetings from the children before me,

I seemed to forget any concerns I may have had about saying "the right thing," whatever that may have been. Instead, I just shared with them my story. I shared that when I was a little girl, about their age, I lost the sight in my right eye in twenty-four hours. I shared about getting my driver's license and being an avid basketball player, even though I could only see out of one eye. I then briefly explained that my vision loss was caused by my retinas detaching. I shared that my left eye started to do exactly what my right eye had already done. I shared about the battle I had fought for over six years to save what little sight I still had. I shared about the thirteen operations I under-went, desperately clutching at the hope that each would help save my vision. I shared how I did eventually lose that war during one of the surgeries, and of how I woke up in the recovery room completely blind at the age of thirty-five.

I then asked the children to close their eyes to give them an idea of what it would be like to move through their day with no sight at all. I asked the kids what kinds of challenges they thought they may face, and their answers were honest, sincere, and full of an earnest desire to understand. I realized that these children, after having met me and walked away with this new knowledge, will never see a blind child the same way again. That maybe, just maybe, because of our time together, this group of children will see that blind boy or girl as just another kid on the playground with all the same likes and dislikes as themselves. Maybe they would reach out and befriend that blind classmate and embrace his or her differences instead of separating themselves because of their uncertainty and doubt.

Then something happened to me that unexpectedly brought tears to my eyes. I thought about my younger brother, David, for the first time in a very long time. My childhood came rushing back to me in a blur of pain and sorrow, as I remembered how my little brother was bullied and made fun of because of his speech impediment. He was born with a cleft palate, a hole in the roof of his mouth that was repaired when he was a few months old, but his speech patterns were very difficult for people to understand. He went to speech therapy for years, but through those years, he was mercilessly teased.

I remember sticking up for him on the playground at school and telling the kids to leave him alone. He came home crying almost every day. It broke my heart to watch the ruthless treatment take the joy out of school for David. Standing there that morning in that local elementary school room witnessing the light-bulbs of understanding coming on in the hearts and minds of those fourth graders made me think about how different my brother's school career could have been had we had A Touch of Understanding to help the other kids better understand my brother's situation.

So many things slid into place for me that morning, feeling for the first time in over twenty-one months, and perhaps a whole lifetime, like I had found my equilibrium. Being there with those children, with their honesty and eagerness to know truths otherwise denied to them, I realized that I did indeed know how I was moving through my life as a blind person. That it was one day, no, one moment at a time, and as long as I stood in that truth, the truth that was becoming clearer and clearer to me as I continued to speak, as I so honestly laid my life out for these kids, I realized that everything was going to be alright. That I was going to be alright.

We repeated our talks once more that morning for the next group of fourth graders, and I found that I had already improved on my delivery just in the time it took to do a second run. After the workshops were finished for the day, all the volunteers met again in the multipurpose room, where Leslie and the crew were now busy deconstructing all the stations to load into ATOU's trailer. Leslie made a point to come up to me and ask how it went. I'm pretty sure I was beaming. I told her that I loved it. I admitted to having been a bit nervous, because I didn't know what to expect, but that the kids made it so easy that my nerves just fell away as I told my story.

I told her that the students' questions were so amazing and insightful, that it was so much fun helping them to better understand blindness and what it is like to live with a disability. Leslie then shared with me something that blew me away. She told me that she had already gotten feedback from not only the kids as they gleefully told her all about me and what they learned, but from the teachers who had also heard my talks. Leslie told me that the teachers had been moved and heartened by my story, and how amazing I was in my honesty and interaction with the kids. Apparently, I was all the buzz!

Now I want to stop and say that this feedback, although it was brand new to me and it filled my heart with joy, was not then and has never been, exclusive to only me. What I want you to understand is that this is the impact we, the speakers, have on the lives of the students. When children are given the opportunity to hear the truth about someone's life, and it's presented in a warm, friendly, and humorous delivery, they are given permission to open their hearts and let us in. It is only when this happens that the truth of our shared human experience is able to enter in, and the social barriers that have been established between us come tumbling down.

That is what happened that first morning for me and the kids I addressed in that classroom. We connected on a level that broke down all the predetermined obstacles that exist between sighted and blind human beings. For the space of the workshops, there was nothing between us, and they knew that as much as I did. And this is when I began to heal. It wasn't the praise of Leslie's words that made me proud; it was that I was able to "reach" through the veil and connect with my fellow human beings in a way that none of us would ever forget.

This is the magic that is A Touch of Understanding. In that moment, I realized that what Leslie was saying to me, as she gave me such glowing feedback, was that what happened between me and the kids was not about me at all. It was so much bigger than that. It was bigger than just one person making a contribution, and that the combined efforts of both the speakers and the volunteers working the stations created a life-altering transformation into the realm of acceptance and understanding.

Unsurprisingly, I was hooked and the rest, as they say, is history. That morning launched my career with A Touch of Understanding. That was in August of 2000, and I have been associated in one way or another with this amazing organization ever since. It's like what they say about stray animals, that once you feed them, they never leave. Well, ATOU feeds me in so many ways that I could never even fathom the idea of leaving.

Soon after that benchmark of a morning, I became one of the regular speakers for ATOU. I got to meet the famous Mike Penketh*, who is the speaker I understudied for that morning, and we became the dynamic duo. He had an amazing canine companion named Magy, and she went with him to every workshop. The kids loved them both. Before I knew it, I was at

*Mike Penketh, see page 34

Guide Dogs for the Blind in San Rafael in July of 2001, as it was time for me to partner up with my own four-legged companion. Callahan, my eighty-five pound black Labrador retriever joined the ATOU team that August, and we never looked back. I was easily able to incorporate what it was like to have a guide dog by my side, and all that he brought to my life into my speeches. The students all fell in love with him, just as I had, and it only enriched my presentations.

As a speaker with ATOU, I have spoken to hundreds of students in many situations, but there was one day that stands out in my mind as a show-stopper. We were presenting our workshop to a small group of students attending school on an Indian reservation. When it was my turn to speak, I asked a question to the children who were all fanned out in a half circle on the floor in front of me, "Do you know anyone who is blind?"

The youngest little one in the group, who was comfortably seated on her teacher's lap, raised her hand and shouted out, "Oh, I do! I do!"

Calling on her, I questioned again, "You know someone who is blind?" And she said with the greatest of pride, "Yes, Hannah is blind." There was a small murmur among the group of kids, as the teacher said, "No honey, Hannah is not blind, Hannah is blonde."

With that, the ATOU speakers, staff members, volunteers, various employees, and representatives of the casino exploded into laughter. She had been so sincere, and that made it even sweeter. After we all caught our breath and did our best to reign ourselves back in to continue, I told her that I understood what she was trying to say, because there were times when I had my "blind" moments, and then there were times when I had my "blonde" moments. The room went up again, and it was minutes later before the next speaker could take the floor. It was a great moment for all of us, and one that allowed everyone to come together in shared understanding and acceptance. It was definitely one of my favorite moments of all time.

If I'm being completely honest, my life was re-launched that morning in August of 2000, when I stood in front of those students for the first time. The opportunity to be a speaker with ATOU came along at a time in my life when my world had been turned upside down and sideways. What ATOU does for its speakers is to give us the opportunity to talk about what is going on in our lives as it pertains to our disability and, for many of us, this is a new development that we have to get used to.

Talking to the kids about my blindness helped me to explain it to myself. I think this is true for a lot of us. Though having been on the ATOU Board of Directors for many years now, when I periodically get the chance to step back into the classroom as a speaker, and I tell my story to the kids, it's as if I'm reinforcing for myself who I really am and what I am capable of accomplishing. When I tell the kids about losing my sight, the things I do and the tools I use to accomplish my goals, I get the chance to tell myself that I do indeed have all that I need to be successful in my own life.

Because of what we do, children like my brother can feel accepted and valued as the precious spirits they are. Thank you, Leslie, for giving us all this gift of clarity.

"We fear what we don't understand."

—*Andrew Smith*

Linda Otley

ATOU Founding Board President

The need for teaching understanding had been present long before we ever began A Touch of Understanding.

Linda Otley

It had been in the collective conscious of anyone who ever saw or felt the pain of being teased, isolated, or separated from others because of a difference. Leslie had seen this in her childhood with her aunt. I had experienced it with my own challenge in recovering from the results of Polio. We saw and felt it daily in our school environment as we worked with students. Parents felt this with their children. It was our students who felt the lonely pain. In fact, the pain could be with those who teased or with those who were being teased. Either way, it separated them from the possibility of knowing and accepting one another.

In the early 1990s, I was a special education teacher at Greenhills School in the Eureka Union School District. I had the privilege of working with a wonderful staff, who sought to create an environment in which all students would feel accepted and respected. Yet, our students with perceived differences often felt alone and unaccepted.

It was Leslie DeDora who felt the need to do something more. She believed that she could create a program to break down barriers and reduce the fear that exists in us all. She wanted to make a difference through fostering acceptance and understanding through a program that would be called A Touch of Understanding. She had the idea that if students could see how we are all alike, and build an understanding of the challenges faced by people with perceived disabilities, then awareness and acceptance might be the outcome. In fact, it would possibly create inclusion. It would be a tall order.

Leslie shared her excitement and her ideas with a few teachers and aides at our school. She was encouraged by our principal to go after her dream. We were her supporters. Initially, there were seven of us who gathered at Leslie's home: Pat Covey, our school secretary, was one of the participants. Pat was the face of our school as she greeted all who came through our office. She worked with parents, students, and all staff. She worked closely with our nurse and Principal Clara Taylor, who joined us in showing her support for the program. Ruby Rodina, who worked in our resource room, also participated. She made sure that teachers throughout our district had the materials and curriculum resources they needed. Included in the initial seven was Ann Mallo*, a second grade teacher who worked with many of my special needs students in the regular educational setting, and she was a wonderful resource. And, finally, Joan Karr, an amazing aide who worked with me in my classroom. Leslie was an aide in Ann Mallo's second grade class and also worked in my class with a specific child.

I was the Special Day Class Teacher, and I worked with all the teachers as students would be mainstreamed into their

*Annmarie Mallo, see page 16

classes. I also worked with parents, both from my class and those I met through the student study team process. I, like the others, was excited about the possibilities in Leslie's dream. Leslie's dad, Ed, was also there. He enthusiastically supported Leslie and jumped in to help with anything and everything. He has continued his support throughout the years.

Leslie was dedicated to beginning the process of making A Touch of Understanding a reality. She decided to quit her job as a classroom aide. She had no guarantees where this great idea would go. She had no financial security and NO pay. She took a leap of faith as she stepped in to her calling. She believed that together we could get this program started. However the truth of the matter was that we had no experience, and our learning curve was steep.

We needed to know how to become a non-profit organization. We knew that we needed the basics to form a non-profit board. So we elected a secretary, a treasurer, and a president. I was the president those first few years. We worked to create a mission statement and shared ideas of how we might get the donations we needed. There was a lot of brainstorming in those early days. Leslie and Ed did most of the program work. They developed the program and sought out the materials and, of course, the much-needed volunteers.

It was a gift to us all when Taymour Ravandi became involved. He was an attorney for Protection and Advocacy, Inc., a non-profit that provided legal assistance to people with disabilities. He provided us with real guidance and attended our board meetings. He also was a huge inspiration. I may have forgotten to mention that Taymour is blind.

Leslie and Ed did the outreach. They presented to the Lion's Club, Rotary, and any organization that might provide community support and funds. The Greenhills Parent Club provided early support to bring the program to all of our nine second grade classrooms on our Greenhills campus. Eventually, the program began to broaden to other districts within Placer County. Leslie, with the help of Ed, developed a program that is as much as it is today.

News of ATOU began to spread. In the late 1990s, our board knew that for ATOU to grow, we needed to encompass people who had more knowledge, time, and background in non-profits. It was hard to let go, but necessary. We didn't know at that time how it would be. I realize now that we all experienced the start.

The mission was to encourage acceptance and respect for all individuals, and to minimize discrimination and misunderstandings experienced by children and adults. What an honor to have been there at the beginning and to see how Leslie's big idea continues to grow. It has become not just Leslie's Big idea, but a family of volunteers and community that eagerly embrace and encourage others.

AND so it goes.....and so it goes. Thank you to all of those who have continued to work in ATOU Board positions and to all of the volunteers. I am so grateful and amazed at seeing students become involved in the Youth F.O.R.C.E. Thank you, Leslie, for this opportunity. You are a beautiful gift to the world. No one can ever really know how their awareness, acceptance, and action will play out in the future.

"I believe that man will not merely endure: he will prevail."

—William Faulkner

Mike Penketh

ATOU Speaker

Remember those ol' science fiction flicks that talked about the future, the twilight zone, everything from wristwatch communicators, time machines, to space travel? In a way, ATOU works in the twilight zone: we kind of work in the future, because kids are our future. I always stress the importance of staying in school, of getting a good education. I tell "my kids," you are my future; you are the doctors, engineers, teachers who will run my country, and I want smart leaders. Stay in school! If you give a kid a small amount of extra time with patience today, he'll remember it, and decades down the road he will do the same and the world will be better.

Mike Penketh in his custom-designed aerobatic airplane

Those of you who don't know me: I am a retired captain who flew for Air Cal and American Airlines, VA-retired Captain, United States Marine Corps, and a Naval aviator, and I'm married to the wonderful Mary Ann.

Disabled? Yes I am. In September 1993, three days after winning the biplane class at the Reno National Air Races, I lost both hands in an auto accident. I lived in the fast lane—the only place for me to live. In the auto accident I speak of, I was going

34

300 mph on the Bonneville Salt Flats. Boys and girls—that is the fast lane!

So, why did I get involved in ATOU? Simply put, it was for my benefit. I had just returned from a summer flying the aerobatic air show circuit in South Africa (yes—with no hands). During this "safari" I spoke to several schools, on TV, on radio stations, and in newspapers. I was "The Yank" with the funny hands. As a relatively new bilateral amputee, this became tremendous therapy. Upon my return, the therapy continued as I toured the country as a speaker for my prosthetics company, and meeting other amputees.

Soon I was home, having coffee, reading the paper and looking for the sports section. The front page of the second section of *The Sacramento Bee* was dedicated to ATOU, and I read the entire page. Remembering the therapy I had received from speaking in South Africa … mmm … maybe I can benefit from this program? At the end of the article was a contact phone number, so the following Monday, I met with Leslie and her dad, Ed, at Caffe Italia in Davis, California. It seems like yesterday, but that was seventeen years and about 2,000 presentations ago—yes it is an addiction. Let's add it up: I live about fifty miles, and an hour's drive, one way, from each presentation— maybe I've driven about 200,000 miles and spent about 500 hours on the road the past seventeen years. And it's worth every mile and second.

I wanted to do more than instruct in the activity stations. So, I suggested to Leslie and Ed that I take half the kids, show a video, answer questions and then trade with the kids doing the activities. Like magic, the speaker portion of ATOU was born. After working with the kids, seeing their attitudes, feelings, and understanding change before my eyes, I realized I had stumbled into another world. Soon, we had several more disabled volunteers to tell their valuable personal stories and experiences. Several volunteers soon bloomed to twenty to thirty volunteers giving two to three presentations a day, two-plus days a week.

Now the secret I am so proud of. Just as I've seen the kids change, I have seen the same changes in our speakers. We have given these volunteers who have disabilities a chance to share who they are, a chance to lead a twenty- to thirty-minute presentation, a chance to lead a question/answer session, a chance to feel important and needed. These special volunteers make me proud; we need them.

When I speak to the kids, I always stress education. Go to high school; go to college. Get a good education, and all the doors of life will be open: no education means some of those doors will remain locked. I use myself as an example. College got me commissioned in the Marine Corps, which led to being a Naval aviator. A fantastic life, supersonic single engine/seat jets, aircraft carriers, and a government gas credit card in my pocket. That experience got me my dream job as an airline captain. But wait a minute, things don't always happen as fast as we like.

While waiting for my dream job, I had more fun than anyone in the world. The winters found me on the ski slopes, or on my sailboat in San Diego. The summers found me in the left seat, flying fire bombers, which opened a new world—a world of even more adventure. I worked/toured Central and South America, flying a research project in the only four-engine PBY aircraft in the world. The following winter (1978), I found myself in Honduras. Sitting on the runway, and still having fun with my right hand on the stick and my left hand on the throttle, cleared for takeoff in one of the last combat-ready F4U Corsairs. Although the Corsair was a single-seat fighter plane, I always had a copilot. My dad, who passed a long time ago, was a WWII, Korean War Marine, and his airplane of choice was the Corsair. Every time I climbed into the cockpit, I felt his presence.

Back to the real world, the airlines, and that dream job. My first flight as a B737 first officer for Air Cal (based in Newport Beach—a tough life). I met a flight attendant with a special gleam in her eye. Mary Ann has been by my side ever since; throughout my darkest times, she has never wavered. I got that dream job not knowing it came with such wonderful baggage. I am a fortunate man.

I have to admit there has been another woman in my life. While Mary Ann maintained our home life, a cute little blonde kept me busy; she attended more than 1,500 ATOU presentations with me, and more than 50,000 kids got to pet her. This was Magy, my golden retriever service dog, my 24/7 companion, my shadow. She passed away in 2015 at fifteen years, eight months, and two days old. If any of you are disabled and have not explored life with a service dog, you might be cheating yourself out of an outstanding experience. As I said, Magy was my shadow; she knew her job was me.

Soon after Magy arrived, we saw the sport of dog agility on TV. I thought it looked fun, and lessons began. About two years later, we entered our first agility competition. The next five+ years, we probably spent three weekends a month in the agility ring, and an entire new life opened up for us. Weekdays were for the kids, weekends Magy became an agility champion. She earned about fifty titles and two championships. Magy is the only known service dog to earn an agility championship, and together we are the only known disabled handler/service dog to achieve that status.

For young men and women reading this, I have a few suggestions. 1. Go to school, 2. No drugs, 3. Easy on the alcoholic drinks, 4. You will get a good job because you went to school, 5. That good job may lead to a partner like Mary Ann, and 6. Stay out of debt. Remember you were put on this world to be successful, not to fail. With a good education, you can make things happen. Don't wait for things to happen, get out there and make them happen! You can do anything you want, if you want it bad enough.

*Mike Penketh's book, *Within my Grasp: A Double Amputee's True Story,* is available on Amazon.

"The most beautiful thing we can experience is the mysterious. It is the source of all true art and science."

—Albert Einstein

Michael Wilson

Member of the ATOU Board of Directors

I was first exposed to A Touch of Understanding during my year as president of the Granite Bay Rotary Club in 1996/1997.

Michael Wilson

During my tenure in Rotary, I listened to a myriad of presentations, but none captivated my imagination like the one I heard that day. After the meeting, I spoke with Leslie DeDora and Ed Ennis, the father and daughter dynamo who founded ATOU. Leslie gave me even more insight into the inner workings of the program and invited me to watch a workshop. I gladly accepted the invitation and, soon after, I met her and Ed at a local elementary school to watch the team in action. I was mesmerized! Over the course of about three hours, I witnessed something that made a profound impact on me—change!

In the beginning of the presentation, I recall seeing the young students (third graders, I believe) fidgeting, talking, and behaving like all young students tend to do at a school assembly. Soon Leslie began speaking, and the students quieted down and settled in. Leslie didn't speak at the students, she spoke with them. During Leslie's introduction, she interjected questions such as ("Have you ever felt different from others?" "What makes you sad?"). This opened up a dialogue between the students, and I noticed them becoming more comfortable.

Leslie went on to describe her experiences with her Aunt Betty (who was intellectually disabled), and how she grew to understand her aunt and accept her differences, but she also accepted her similarities. As Leslie continued, she began to describe other disabilities, and how people with disabilities were able to cope with everyday life. I noticed the kids becoming engaged. They raised their hands and began asking questions.

At the conclusion of Leslie's introduction, the students broke into groups and then went to various stations. At that time, the stations consisted of maneuvering wheelchairs through an obstacle course of cones; in the white cane station, the students wore blindfolds and were taught how to navigate with the canes; in a mirror writing station, the students found how hard it was to trace a path on paper while only watching in the mirror (to simulate a learning disability); students learned about Braille writing in another station; and in my favorite station, the orthotics and prosthetics station, students got a chance to handle a variety of braces and artificial limbs. This was an eye-opening experience for the kids. They actually had an opportunity to experience what a disabled person must do on a daily basis from a hands-on perspective.

As the commercial says, "but wait, there's more." After the students went through the stations, they regrouped, and I followed them into a classroom where they were met by two ATOU volunteer speakers who started an interactive discussion about their disabilities. What really struck me was how open and honest the speakers were about their particular disabilities, and they engaged the students with questions and answers. No question was out-of-bounds, and the speakers did a fantastic job of explaining how they coped with everyday life and the challenges that they needed to overcome due to their disabilities.

What was remarkable was that the speakers were able to elicit empathy, rather than pity, as the students began to recognize that people with disabilities were no different than themselves. The speakers just required a set of "tools" that allowed them to negotiate life. At the end of the presentation, all the students assembled in the multipurpose room for some final words from Leslie, and a chance to ask more questions and provide comments. The common sentiment among the students was that they now felt comfortable about people with disabilities, and that they would now look at the person and not the disability— change!

Well, I was hooked! Leslie asked if I would consider joining the Board of Directors, and without hesitation, I said, "yes," and I haven't looked back since. I was very lucky to have had that meeting with Leslie and Ed and becoming part of ATOU.

It's now been about 18 years that I have been involved with ATOU, and I can say without a doubt, the world is a better place with ATOU in it. I have had the privilege to meet and interact with (and call friends) some of the most amazing people. As of this writing, ATOU has affected more than 80,000 students, and countless more who have received the benefits of their exposure to ATOU. I am forever grateful to have "stumbled" across the path of Leslie and Ed, and my view of the world and that of my family has changed (for the better) because of ATOU.

Long-Time Volunteers

"Be joyful in hope, patient in affliction, and faithful in prayer."

—Romans 12:12

Dan Adragna

ATOU Speaker

Not a Leg to Stand On

Life was beginning to feel worth living again. In late 1995, I was a single dad with full custody of my two teenaged children, Ryan and Shelly. We lived in a modest townhome not far from the beach, church, and friends. I was pulling out of a deep depression brought on by divorce, job loss, financial ruin, and loss of our home.

Just before Christmas, I caught the flu. Each day my symptoms worsened. But as the foreman electrician on a high-tech office building project, I had to keep

Dan Adranga

my nose to the grindstone. The job had to be completed before noon December 23, and I certainly wasn't going to disappoint. Only by the grace of God did I make the deadline and, later, a Christmas party. After sitting in a chair for an hour without saying a word or eating, I announced my departure. I honestly have no recollection of the drive home.

I fell into bed and felt about as bad as you can feel without being in a train wreck. I had every flu symptom imaginable. Later that evening, Ryan drove me to the urgent care clinic. The physician alleged I had the flu. We made a stop at the drugstore to fill a prescription, and I crawled back into bed.

On Christmas Eve, I cancelled our plans. I went back to the medical clinic that afternoon. A chest x-ray indicated pneumonia in my right lung. I felt as though I would black out. The combination of pneumonia with the fact I have diabetes was enough to authorize a trip to Dominican Hospital in Santa Cruz. The last thing I recall was being wheeled into the admitting office to answer insurance-related questions. Then the lights went out, and no one was home. I slipped into a deep slumber—and didn't wake for six weeks.

Dangerous bacteria entered my blood system and caused a toxic blood infection called Septic Shock. For good measure, I developed a staphylococcus infection. I was given an assortment of antibiotics and medicines. My heart stopped on four occasions, and each time I was miraculously saved with a defibrillator. I was given dialysis treatments for kidney failure. My body temperature rose to 107 degrees for several days in a row, and I had a markedly elevated white blood cell count. The hospital staff warned my family that even if I awoke from my coma, I would probably be "a vegetable."

By the next morning, pneumonia filled both lungs, preventing me from breathing on my own. My doctors cut a hole in my throat to insert a tracheotomy tube, connecting me to a ventilator. It's likely this procedure caused paralysis to my vocal cords, tongue, and epiglottis. I had several blood transfusions. Due to poor circulation and complications of diabetes, my legs were amputated below my knees to stop gangrene from spreading. It was a living nightmare.

The hospital staff gave my family virtually no hope. On the day I flat-lined twice, Pastor Rene Schlaepfer of Twin Lakes Church was asked to prepare everyone for my death. He and about 50 of my loved ones waited for the inevitable. It never came.

At first I could barely open my eyes. I felt like I was in a bad science-fiction movie as morphine produced strange daydreams and frightening nightmares. Several days passed before I could remain awake for any length of time. My friend Kelly told me about my legs. I remember it clearly. He said, "Your legs had to be removed in order to stop the gangrene from spreading so you could have a chance to live."

My response was, "That's a small price to pay to be alive." I still feel that way today. Sure, it's an inconvenience, and I can't do all I used to do. But I've chosen to focus on what I can do and not dwell on what I can't. Compared to being dead, I'll take walking with prosthetic legs any day!

When I physically came alive for the second time in my life, I weighed 85 pounds. I looked down at my chest and saw nothing but skin on bone. Having paralyzed vocal cords meant I had to receive nourishment through feeding tubes. It also meant I had no voice—barely a faint whisper. To communicate, I was given an alphabet board to point out letters as my deformed fingers couldn't grasp a pen.

The constant flow of family and friends encouraged me. Pastors and people I didn't know from church came by to pray daily. My room was filled with balloons, cards, flowers, pictures, posters, books, and Rene's sermon tapes. Not only was I encouraged, but inspired, and explored why God chose to save me.

After spending nearly four months in the hospital and a rehab center, I was taken to the house I grew up in. It felt good to be home. After everything I'd been through, living with Mom and Dad was a treat. My mode of transportation became a manual wheelchair.

In November 1996, I was fit with prosthetic legs. Having bought a car with hand controls, I started to regain my independence. Since I could no longer work as an electrician, I attended college—something I'd always wanted. I finished my bachelor's degree at San Jose State University, while volunteering in the disability ministry. I had the privilege of beginning and leading the special-needs ministry of Bayside Church in Roseville, called Through the Roof.

I'm often asked if I ever get depressed or if I'd change anything. My answer is always, "Not a chance." Considering I should've died, how can I be depressed? But I also believe I have an important choice when dealt tough circumstances. I can choose to have a pity party and feel sorry for myself, or I can rise to the challenge and make the best of it. My life now is not perfect, but complete, with a proper perspective, and a meaningful purpose.

Volunteering with A Touch of Understanding has been a true blessing to me. While a challenge initially, it has provided the opportunity to hone my speaking skills and share my story. And, to serve alongside an awesome group of volunteers. My favorite part of the presentation is the Q & A session. The younger students are not afraid to ask anything. And I strongly encourage them to do so—no question is off limits for me. ATOU is a great program, and has made a huge impact on the lives of participants AND volunteers.

Currently, I also direct the Sacramento office of Joni and Friends, a non-profit, faith-based organization that ministers to people affected by disability—both locally and globally. I also led "Through the Roof," the disability outreach at Bayside Church in Granite Bay, California.

"Minds are like parachutes. They only function when they are open."
—Sir James Dewar

Joyce Beeman

ATOU Workshop Activity Instructor, Member of the ATOU Board of Directors

The notice on the bulletin board at the library said, "Volunteers who enjoy working with children needed for school presentations. Contact Leslie DeDora, telephone (916) 791-4146."

I was looking for some sort of volunteer work that I would enjoy and could fill some of my time since I was newly retired. I had attended a breakout session at a Woman's Business Conference that recommended that

Joyce Beeman

you choose volunteer work that gave you a lot in return. "Don't stuff envelopes if what you want to do is write press releases. Every non-profit has a need for all sorts of skills."

Having been an elementary school teacher, I knew I could work well with children. I called Leslie, and we had an interesting and friendly phone conversation. Leslie asked me about my background and what I enjoyed doing. I explained that I was a former teacher, had been training technical people for a large computer company, and that during my last seven years of employment I was a technical writer and developer of computer training courses, as well as creating requests for proposals and feasibility studies for the State of California.

"I have just the job for you," she said. She explained that ATOU needed a volunteer manual written to explain the tasks for each volunteer and at each workshop activity station. She invited me to see a workshop before I began writing.

I began right away and started volunteering one or two days a week, which was the number of days per week that workshops were provided in 2002. I soon was recruited to join the ATOU Board of Directors. In addition to workshop volunteering and board work, I wrote several winning grants to bring needed funds to the organization. I became Leslie's unpaid staff member. She now has several staff members as the organization has grown considerably in the past twelve years. To date, workshops have been given to more than 80,000 students. Now, twelve years after the start, I volunteer twice a month to help with workshops. I can lead all the activity stations, except one, for which I have not been trained. I also fill in for Leslie to facilitate the program occasionally, as well as doing other ad hoc tasks.

Why do I continue to volunteer for this group as well as

making regular financial contributions? I have seen first-hand the value of this program to all the students who participate. I have seen the value to the speakers who have disabilities and share their experiences with students. Also, I have seen the very important benefit to classmates with disabilities as their fellow students get a better understanding of what it is like to have a disability. I have made friends with some of the most amazing people, both with and without a disability.

I have heard comments such as:

"Wow, I didn't know that Tommy could do all those things!"

"My blind neighbor says that you people at A Touch of Understanding could change the world."

"I will never tease someone who is different from me again."

I am a strong believer in the need for character education to raise good, kind, and capable people. A Touch of Understanding is one way to help increase the exposure young people have to folks that may be a bit different, and for them to realize that these people have much to contribute, just as they do. I like to see those students wearing the ATOU button that says "I choose to be kind."

"In the end, it's not going to matter how many breaths you took, but how many moments took your breath away."

—*Shing Xiong"*

Jackie Callahan

ATOU Workshop Activity Instructor and Volunteer
Administrative Assistant

"Wow!" "Way cool!" "That's amazing!" "No Way!"

These are a few of the comments I hear as I share a hands-on experience introducing orthotic and prosthetic devices to school children. It is exciting to watch as their expressions of discomfort change as they get "up close and personal" with the tools used by those with disabilities.

Jackie Callahan

It all started with a broken ankle in 2000. While using a wheelchair, I had a chance to see how inaccessible our accessible society really is. This was also an opportunity to experience how uneducated and ill-informed the public is regarding people with special needs.

In the spring of 2001, Leslie and I were involved with the Sacramento office of Joni and Friends. I noticed a strange thing happening every Thursday and Friday morning: Leslie would disappear. Being curious, I asked her about it. She told me a little bit about ATOU and, of course, invited me to "come observe a workshop." Thus began this fifteen-year adventure.

What prepared me for THIS?

- I was born early in the morning: Great for those o'dark thirty workshop times.

- I was a Girl Scout and worked as a camp counselor: Great way to learn to "be prepared."
- I drove a mobile canteen (roach coach): Great way to meet lots of "interesting people" and get driving experience.
- I worked for Sprouse-Reitz variety store: Great for setting up displays and "making nice with people."
- I was a head cashier at Laurentide Finance: Great for "learning the books" and handling money and staff.
- I ran a print shop for a non-profit (with off-set press, folders, trimmers, collators): Great for learning graphic arts.
- I worked in the office at Ozark Trucking, and was a member of the safety committee: Great for learning payroll, scheduling, problem solving, and customer relations.
- I have volunteered at a camp for girls since 1964, as director, activity specialist, and board member: Great for leadership training and relationships.
- I worked with Joni & Friends (international disability ministry) as an office assistant: Great for organization, dealing with finances, and learning about people with special needs.
- I have been with ATOU since the spring of 2001. Now I see why I had all those other experiences!

There are so many stories of growth, new confidence, and changed lives among the students and the volunteers. It is a privilege to be involved in this worthwhile endeavor.

"The most important thing is to enjoy your life—to be happy—that's all that matters."

—*Audrey Hepburn*

JDD Doran-Jammer

ATOU Speaker

My body didn't use vitamin A properly, a very uncommon problem. When I was around four years old, the doctors discovered that I had enough vitamin A in my body for three adults. Normally, vitamin A helps our eyes. But my body had stored so much vitamin A, possibly starting before I was born, that it caused a brain tumor that damaged my optic nerves, which connect the eyes to the brain. I ate no carrots, tomatoes, and other vitamin A-rich foods for a couple of years, and the brain tumor went away, but the damage to my optic nerves was permanent. My body now uses vitamin A properly.

JDD Doran-Jammer

Not seeing color and seeing unrecognizable blurs has been natural for me since I was around three years old, before I knew the names of colors. So, if I were to regain sight now, in my forties, it would take more than a few years to learn to live with sight, just as it is easier for children than for adults to adjust to becoming blind.

Actually, I have some contrast vision in my right eye, so I understand light and dark, reflections, and shadows. In many cases, I can't visually distinguish between a shadow and a solid

51

object. I tune out a lot of what I see because, even at normal walking pace, it takes too long for me to try to understand a fraction of the nameless blurs I see.

I don't know why I found it so appealing to learn how to skate, starting with continual falling in the backyard of my foster home when I was around six. At long last, in eighth grade, I got good at making it all the way around the rink at least twice without falling. When I was around sixteen, a skater in a rink kept threatening to give me hospital-grade injuries, because I kept getting too close, and the rinks won't let me use my white cane (because we're going so fast). That scared me. I was betting that if I explained to him that I couldn't properly see him, he would make an issue of keeping me off the rink floor.

In my early twenties, I got to use three bibs from downhill skiing while skating: "blind skier," "ski guide," and "blind." I wanted to give sighted people adequate warning that something quite unusual was happening; I'm very grateful I wore the bib.

In my early thirties, I decided it was time to put my skating together with my white cane skills on the sidewalks in very familiar territory. I'm grateful to Mike Marasso for his message about wearing a helmet. I'm not allowed to wear it in the rink, but it has protected my head against hard—what I call "face plants"—foliage that smacks me in the head (my safety glasses likewise have been useful). I agree with the occasional people on the sidewalks who tell me I'm "crazy" for skating. It's easier for me to ignore distractions of admiration like that when somebody is keeping me company, even if they're only walking quickly or jogging slowly.

In kindergarten, I learned to read and write Braille, while my classmates learned to read and write print. I've learned that even third graders don't remember learning to read and write, so I hope they believe me that it was no harder for me to learn Braille than it was for them to learn print.

At ATOU workshops, students get to practice writing their names in Braille. And, I'm always glad when people tell me how happy the kids look when I read their name for them. Some kids want to know how I drive. I jokingly respond, "I love driving bumper cars, but they won't give me a license."

ATOU's interactive education makes me more interested in responding to people's questions when I'm running errands, such as shopping, and banking. Often, I interrupt what I'm doing so I can educate strangers about my disability. I enjoy watching how my interaction in public directly affects what I say while presenting for ATOU.

"To men, a man is but a mind. Who cares what face he carries or what form he wears?"

—Ambrose Bierce

Greg Elie
ATOU Speaker

I was born with congenital hydrocephalus. My mother found out about my condition when she was seven-and-a-half months pregnant from an ultrasound picture that showed my head was abnormally large for that stage of her pregnancy.

While still pregnant with me, my mom was sent to UCLA Medical Center in Los Angeles for high-risk pregnancies. The

Greg Elie

53

doctors at UCLA decided to try an experimental surgery to correct my condition while I was still in the womb. At that time, fetal surgery was on the cutting edge of technology. They performed two brain surgeries, to relieve the pressure on my brain, while I was still inside my mother's womb. I was the first baby in California to have this surgery and the first baby in the world to survive. I had other complications at birth, including epilepsy, vision problems, hearing loss, and scoliosis. Altogether, I have had fifteen surgeries to correct many of these problems.

My early challenges were learning to do basic functions, such as sitting up, crawling, and walking. I went to an early intervention program at UCLA for children with disabilities where we were taught, using special devices, how to strengthen our bodies to perform these skills. I used to sit in a corner box to strengthen my back muscles, which helped me learn to sit up. I practiced crawling using a carpet roll under my stomach supporting my body, which helped me to stay on my knees. I used a child-size walker to help me walk. As I got older, I think the hardest thing for me was my balance problem. I never learned to ride a bike or skateboard. (But, I do ride bikes and skateboards in my video games.) I used to play Challenger Baseball, which is baseball for kids with disabilities. I have no directional sound, since I'm deaf in my left ear, but I've learned to adapt by asking people where they are.

One of my biggest challenges was in my junior year of high school. That year, I had three surgeries and had to miss a lot of school. One of the surgeries I had was for my scoliosis, and I had to wear a body cast twenty-three hours a day for six months to straighten my spinal cord after a ten-hour surgery. That was really uncomfortable. The only time I could take my brace off was for one hour a day to take a shower. I also had a spinal cord surgery and two eye surgeries that year.

I continue to see specialists every six months. I have an MRI every two years to check my shunt, which is a flexible tube surgically placed in the ventricle of my brain. The end of the shunt is in my abdominal cavity, and the shunt drains the excess spinal fluid that accumulates in my brain. Sometimes the shunt malfunctions and has to be replaced. I've had eight shunt revisions so far. In 2009, I had three brain surgeries in one-and-a-half months. I was in rehabilitation for one month where I learned how to walk again.

As long as I take medication every day, my seizures are controlled. I am capable of doing almost everything. Some things, like cutting my nails, are difficult because I have fine motor problems. This also affects my writing, but I use a computer as much as I can.

I graduated from Granite Bay High School in 2001. While I was there, I was mainstreamed in almost all of my classes, and I was allowed to use note-takers to help me. I was given extra time to take my tests. I earned three degrees from Sierra College in Administration of Justice in May of 2006. One was for an AA in Courts, one for an AA in Corrections, and one for an AA in Law Enforcement.

After finishing college, I took a fifty-one hour course at the Rocklin Police Department Volunteer Academy. I've helped them log evidence, assisted in SWAT team exercises for crowd control, and helped with community relations at different schools. I've been on ride-a-longs with police officers and I've helped to maintain squad cars with pertinent information and supplies.

My family found out about ATOU from Leslie DeDora when my mother was a member of the CAC (Community Advisory Committee) for the Loomis School District. My mom was very impressed with the program. I joined ATOU as a volunteer in 2006, after Leslie saw an article about me in the *Granite Bay View*. Leslie contacted our family, and I've been with ATOU ever since.

In addition to ATOU, I am now working at Johnson Ranch Racquet Club (JRRC). Alta Regional Center of California and Progressive Employment Concepts helped me to find this job. I have a job coach who periodically checks on my progress. She communicates with my supervisor for any special needs that I may require. Soon, I will be on my own. The things I do at JRRC include checking in members, handing out locker keys and towels, and answering phones at the front desk. I also gather and wash towels from around the club. If any members have questions, I try to get the information they need.

Working with A Touch of Understanding has been an incredible experience for me. I've been able to share my story with children, and make them more aware of people with disabilities and how to act towards them. I tell them that we are not that different and we all like the same things, even though disabled people may have to do some things differently. I encourage students to never doubt what they can accomplish if they put their minds to it, and tell them how important education is in helping them reach their goals. My motto for everyone is: FOCUS on what you CAN DO…not on what you CANNOT DO! Find another way to do the things that are difficult for you, and always remember it's OK to be DIFFERENT!

ATOU has been as valuable to me as I think it is to the students. I've met so many wonderful people who have so many life experiences to share. I believe we open the eyes of the students in a way no textbook ever could. The "hands-on" experience with the wheelchairs, canes, Braille cards, assistive devices, mirror boards, and the messages of the presenters are life-changing for these students. In my opinion, A Touch of Understanding is an incredible disability-awareness program that should be presented nationwide.

"Whenever you are asked if you can do a job, tell 'em, "Certainly, I can!" Then get busy and find out how to do it."

—Theodore Roosevelt

Courtney Osiow

ATOU Speaker and Member of the ATOU Youth F.O.R.C.E.

Courtney Osiow

I was born a healthy happy baby, even though I was born two weeks late, in March 1992. In the first six months, my parents saw me favoring my left hand and barely using my right hand, but they didn't think anything of it, they just thought "okay, she'll be left handed." At a doctor's appointment for an ear infection, my mom mentioned that I was using my left hand way more than my right. The doctor said that until babies are two, they shouldn't favor either hand and suggested an MRI.

The MRI showed that I had a stroke shortly before or at birth and that I had a disability called hemiplegia, in which one side

57

of your body is weaker than the other. In my case, my right arm and leg are weaker. At first, my parents weren't sure what they needed to do. At the time, the only disability that they knew about was being in a wheelchair, and they just wanted to get whatever equipment I needed to be successful growing up. My pediatrician told my parents that they needed to make sure that I used my right side so I wouldn't neglect it. When we went out, they held my right hand so I would have to look up to my right to see them. The doctor gave me a prescription for physical therapy.

I have a hand brace, so my hand is not in a tight fist all the time, and a leg brace to help me walk. Since my right leg is weaker, I do not walk heel to toe, like an unaffected person walks. I walked high on my right toe, not putting my heel on the ground. The leg braces helped me put my heel down first.

Growing up, I never felt different from my friends. Sure, I couldn't do certain things the way other people did them, but I found different ways to do them. I first heard of A Touch of Understanding when I was in second grade, and they were presenting at my elementary school. My mom wasn't sure how I would react to a "disability awareness" program, so she came along to watch with me. We loved it so much that ever since then we have been involved with ATOU. When I was thirteen, I was able to volunteer as a speaker, because I was being homeschooled.

My message when I speak to the kids has always been that you can do anything you set your mind to—you may just have to come up with a different way to do it. When I was seventeen, I got my driver's license. However, I don't drive like most people. I have a left foot accelerator so I can use my left foot. I have a steering knob to help me turn, and I have a big rear-view mirror to help see what's behind me better.

If someone asked me if I would change anything, or if I wished I didn't have a disability, I wouldn't change a thing. I have met so many people, and I've done so many things because of my disability.

When I was nine, I went to a volunteer picnic for ATOU where Mike Penketh* had his service dog, Magy, who was a release dog from Canine Companions for Independence. Even though Magy had been released from Canine Companions because she chewed on her foot, Mike kept up her training and used Magy as his service dog. I played with Magy all day at the picnic. Mike told my parents that I could get a service dog from Canine Companions for Independence. So we applied and when I was ten, I was matched with my first service dog, Lucey.

I've had three service dogs from Canine Companions, Lucey, Fern, and my new dog, Lolly. Lolly helps me hold things, opens doors using the push plate, and picks up things when I drop them. Lolly can go anywhere I go. She can go to the grocery store, to college with me, even to work with me at the Roseville Police Department.

A Touch of Understanding has been a part of my life for almost as long as I can remember. That's where I first met Mike and Magy, and heard Mike, who lost both hands in a race car accident, talk about his disability. I remember being amazed that even though he'd lost his hands, he was still able to drive, and even fly airplanes again. Through ATOU, I've met many successful people with disabilities over the years. I think that has had a big impact on shaping my feelings about having a disability, and made me see very early that my disability didn't have to limit what I could do.

*Mike Penketh, see page 34

I love speaking with students at ATOU presentations and answering their questions. I even got my best friend Paige Whitefield** to become a speaker, too. Now there are lots of kids speaking. You hear a lot about bullying these days, and sometimes I'm asked if I was ever bullied at school. I never was, and I think that having ATOU presenting to students at schools I attended is largely the reason.

While ATOU positively impacts the lives of kids with disabilities at the schools that are fortunate enough to have ATOU workshops, I've also seen the dramatic ways in which it shifts the perceptions of kids without disabilities. As an ATOU speaker, I've seen that being able to participate in the sessions, and to hear and ask questions of our speakers, helps kids understand that we all have strengths and we all have weaknesses, and that these differences are what make each of us who we are. I think ATOU helps students view differently whatever difficulties they may be having, and it empowers them. I see this same empowered attitude in the kids that participate in ATOU's Youth F.O.R.C.E. I love being part of the Core Planning Group for the Youth F.O.R.C.E., helping plan and participate in all the activities.

I'm in college now, and I have an internship with the Roseville Police Department, so I'm not able to volunteer as a speaker with ATOU or help out in the office anymore. I still feel like part of the ATOU family, though, and the experiences I've had and friendships I've made at ATOU will be with me forever.

**Paige Whitefield, see page 94

"Each friend represents a world in us, a world possibly not born until they arrive, and it is only by this meeting that a new world is born."
—Anais Nin

Karen Parsegian
ATOU Speaker

Karen Parsegian

Life is so not boring. Sometimes, it will throw you a curve. And other times, a crabapple. Smack dab in the middle of your left eye. Had my head been 1/16th of an inch in any other direction that summer night when I was eleven years old, I may never have thought to find my purpose through volunteering, or known any of the funny, kind, strong, resilient, brave, wacky, and wonderful people at A Touch of Understanding, who I am proud to call my friends.

You know something good is happening when students ask insightful, thought-provoking questions that crackle like electricity moments after you've done your talk, want a picture, a hug, or just keep hanging out instead of running off to lunch or recess.

Going totally blind thirty-three years after that childhood accident was a big surprise. Had I known, I would have paid much closer attention (and owned at least one really hot car.) I'm told that few people who have blunt force trauma or lose one eye will ever go blind in the other eye. Apparently, the condition known as sympathetic opthalmyia that affected my perfectly healthy right eye is a one in a million occurrence. Six weeks after the removal of the injured left eye for pain in 2000, my body started attacking itself. High doses of steroids and chemotherapy could not get my immune system to settle down. In the future, anything medically related to my eyes would be a remote possibility, because my right eye was removed in June 2015, so I am fresh out of parts. I now sport a pair of Caribbean-inspired spectacularly warm ocean water blue prosthetic eyes that feel great and often fool many people also standing in line for lattes at Starbuck's on those early ATOU mornings. According to the American Foundation for the Blind only 4 percent of blind people are as blind as I am. No light perception. No shadows. No light. Just dark black—nothing. For an exceptionally visual person like me, whose eye for detail paid the bills, took a little getting used to.

I worked in corporate America and had the good fortune of working with some of the best people at some of the best companies during one of the most exciting times in history. Overnight, out went the IBM Correcting Selectrics with their interchangeable italic font balls, and in came the computers with these corded rodent things that output professional word processing tricks and studio-quality comps right on my desk at the speed of a double click.

This first-hand experience at adapting to seismic change in how one gets things done proved extremely useful in adjusting from a sighted to a blind life. Within two weeks of giving up my car keys, I was going to support groups for the newly blind. I had to relearn how to do absolutely everything, and get used to this new way of seeing the world along with the way people were now treating me. No easy trick. Almost one year to the day I attended an intensive nine-month residential program for independent living at the Colorado Center for the Blind NFB in

Littleton, I learned how to stare down mind-blowing challenges and navigate enigmatic barriers from so many competent people living full lives without sight. Having long-time friend, business associate, and veteran advertising executive Joel Hochberg capture the first eighteen months of my transition (and a wild variety of hairstyles and colors as it is all about the hair, right?) in his very first documentary film *A Daring Adventure* (2004) was like icing on the cake.

If you have to go blind or become disabled, now's a great time as there are more tools and innovations than you can shake a stick at. Here's the thing: tools are just that. They help you do something. While they might look odd to the untrained eye, they do NOT define who you are. Rather, the "how" you do something is the part that is redefined. I'm still a voracious reader only now I use my ears and my hands to experience my favorite black ops/ special forces adventures.

I discovered, however, that the most valuable tools are the ones that never go out of style. They are the ones you can't see. The list is long, beginning with a good attitude and keen sense of humor, grit, sound character, kindness, honesty, empathy, respect, perspective, independence, balance, patience, good organizational and time management skills, stamina, adaptability, focus, perseverance, resilience, commitment to learning, curiosity, creativity, learning to let go and move on, ability to forgive, ability to be forgiven and being useful, productive and helpful to others. All this to simply get back in the game, even when the field is less than level, or it feels like you're swimming upstream.

Speaking of streams, I found myself in one in July 2014 with eight boatloads of ATOU Youth F.O.R.C.E. members, and their families and friends associated with our ATOU crew. Actually, it was the South Fork of the American River on a highly-anticipated, multi-generational overnight camping and whitewater rafting adventure lead by our expert guides at Environmental Traveling Companions. It. Was. A. Blast. It also provides the perfect metaphor for how this ATOU thing works: We may not all be in the same boat, but if you've got to shoot Satan's Cesspool, have an amazing Muriel on the oars sounding the call of the wild with a cool British accent; and have great friends who may happen to be paralyzed hanging onto the chicken strap on your life vest as you get in ready position so that when expert guide Ben confirms the moment to paddle hard for the cliff side photographer's fast action money-shot while shooting the class 3+ rapids, every corpuscle inside your body is prepared to look fabulous and have the time of their lives. Also, should you fall out of the boat, don't swim to shore: smile, roll over onto your back and point your toes downstream so you catch up to the boat. I wonder if it was river running way back in the day that originated that "go with the flow" thing. Hmmm …

For Jill Mason*, Dwight Lunkley**, and me, going with the flow on that 104-degree day was more than just a good idea. It continues to inspire us to see what other kinds of mischief we "Three Amigos" can get into. The bigger, the better. Together, we paint quite the picture. No eyes (me). No arms (Dwight). No legs (Jill). No problemo! Even if you don't see the cowboy, the triathlete, and the humorist, we make a pretty dynamic team. We're incredibly self-sufficient at covering most of the bases wherever we go. Throw in a pizza, or guacamole and chips, well then put the hammer down and we're cooking with gas.

*Jill Mason, see page 181
**Dwight Lunkley, see page 175

I put that trip right up there with tossing out four Major League first pitches, swishing a free throw before a Sacramento Kings vs. Los Angeles Lakers NBA game, and flying on a trapeze with two eyes tied behind my back thirty feet in the air on Santa Monica Pier. The camaraderie and effortlessness of being with so many friends enjoying nature, with everyone pulling their weight to the best of their ability, and that fresh-off-the-grill dinner is just one example of how ATOU tends to eat life while savoring every bite.

While it is true that some folks at ATOU pull more weight than a supply pony navigating Donner Pass in the middle of winter, I can't begin to tell you how cool it is to be part of a group that creates a space and a place that fosters appreciation, independence, inclusion, and best effort. More than "nice," everyone simply "is." It tends to make you want to bring your "A" game to the table. That choosing to be kind thing is more than a tag line on a button. It is a genuine way of life at ATOU.

If I had to sum up the ATOU experience in one thought, it might be this: It's so not a me thing—it's a we thing. And that's why this ATOU thing works. I will be forever thankful to Les, Ann, Rich, and Papa Ed for creating a most precious and brilliant jewel that puts a sparkle in the eye, while enriching so many lives. The feeling you get from being in service to others is priceless. Better than gold, diamonds, and ice cream. (And if you knew me, that ice cream reference is quite the tell!) ATOU is something I shall forever treasure. These people kinda rock.

"Dreams are necessary to life." —Anais Nin

Suzanne Peppers

ATOU Volunteer and Member of the ATOU Advisory Board

"Speakers of ATOU are born ambassadors for good, catalysts for
change, and pioneers for acceptance of things we may not otherwise understand."

Bad news was never my
intended focus. I believe I was
born an optimist. My baby bottle
was never just half-full, but always
full enough. I was a happy child,

Suzanne and Cliff Peppers

living in an Ozzie and Harriet kind of world (for those of you
not old enough to remember them, think "Little House on the
Prairie"). I grew up in the redwood forest of southern Oregon,
where I rarely saw other children. My earliest school memory
was of the one-room schoolhouse, with four combined grades
and a total of about fourteen kids. They pretty much all looked
like me, talked like me, and acted like me.

It was not until we moved to California when I was eight
that I saw children who were "different." I found out that God
made kids with different colors of skin, and I was fascinated. I
suppose I was born to embrace the good in all people, and never
saw differences as flaws.

I landed my very first adult job, at the innocent age of
seventeen, at a television news station, finding myself involved
daily in the woes of our world. You might be surprised to hear that
I loved it! Being the first to know "all things newsworthy" was

thrilling, but understanding the remarkable power of the media to tell the world a story was truly mind-boggling. Mistakenly, I thought I had my finger on the pulse of life and all of its moving parts because each day, working on a newscast, was like reading a new encyclopedia of information. With each story, we learned about the lives of other people, other cultures, medical science, and political differences.

And then, nine years later, when my husband and I welcomed our second son into the world, we both discovered how much we didn't know. "There is a problem," the doctor said. "Your baby is paralyzed. He will never walk, and probably not even sit up." Words we had never heard before were spinning in our heads and breaking our hearts: Spina Bifida, Myleomengeocele, Hydrochephalus. This was our baby. He looked fine to us: a button nose, ten little fingers, and a healthy cry. We knew very little about disabilities and birth defects. Why? I, certainly, should have known more.

Our news bureau should have been telling our viewers about such things. This was life. Real life! Somehow, it all was trumped by wars, and crime, and disasters in other lands. But now, we had our own personal news story happening right here in our lives, and I wanted to know more.

It was my new mission to find stories about parents of babies born with disabilities, and I asked our assignment desk to please cover them. My husband and I worked hard to bring adaptive sports to our city for kids with disabilities who had no other significant outlet to physically express themselves. I used the local news and information media as much as possible to promote such activities, and to encourage understanding about people with disabilities, always hopeful that our able-bodied viewers would see that we are more "alike" than "different" from each other. We are all unique and all living with challenges and gifts—and yet we are all one people.

I left the news business after sixteen years, to independently produce programs for local commercial television and PBS. There comes a time when you must pay attention to who you are, and I knew I was a "good news" person.

As woman of faith, it was clear God had led me down this path—as I was presented with wonderful opportunities to produce videos for organizations like Easter Seals, to help them raise funding and awareness for new therapies, for a disabled sports organization to promote involvement by those with disabilities, and for a care home for adults with Alzheimer's and other disabilities.

I was asked to produce a video for parents about how to prepare their dependent adult child for inter-dependent living away from home. A woman in her twenties (I will call her Julie), had been assigned to be my Assistant Producer on this project. To my surprise, Julie had Downs Syndrome. I learned so much from this wonderful lady.

Several years later, Julie fell ill and was in dire need of a life-saving heart and lung transplant. Her request was denied. The reason? The transplant team felt she would not be able to properly care for herself due to her learning challenges. We all knew that was not the case. Julie held a job, drove a car, lived on her own, and was even an advocate for others with disabilities. "If only they KNEW her, they would understand!" we all bemoaned.

An attorney from a local legal assistance group created to protect the rights of people with disabilities agreed to take on Julie's case pro-bono. He wanted a video produced to help educate the transplant team about Julie and the life she lived. We set about doing just that, calling it "A Day in the Life of Julie." We followed her to an early morning hair appointment, then shopping for a new dress, and finally to a lunch date with her boss and friends. The entire time she was "wired" with a mic. We listened in as she chattered on about her dreams and goals in life. After editing it down to about seven minutes, we shipped the final video "priority/overnight" to both the UCSF and UC San Diego's transplant teams. Within a week, Julie was granted her transplant request and within two months, she had her new heart and lungs.

The power of video to show the reality of the lives of those we don't understand had become an ongoing mission for me. I found it remarkable that in a career full of amazing productions and pretty decent financial contracts, the most meaningful video I ever produced was one I was never paid to produce: the story of Julie. The biggest reward was that a woman who deserved to live a longer life had been given the opportunity to do so— because a video told her story to those who otherwise would never have understood.

Whether disability or just everyday differences, it was my desire to tell the other side of those sad stories we often did for news. As the wife of a deputy sheriff, I could see that my husband's profession was often under scrutiny, and sometimes unfairly represented in the news. It's much more exciting for people to see a bad cop overpowering a citizen than to focus on those who walk old ladies across the street, or wrap their comforting arms around a grieving parent after the death of a child.

69

My husband and I discussed this often over our morning coffee, and proposed a different kind of local television show featuring law enforcement and fire agencies, showing the honorable and brave side of emergency services. This show would focus on the inner workings of those departments, and the real people behind the badge. To produce these stories, we would need to purchase video from local freelance photographers— we called them "stringers" in the business. Some called them "ambulance chasers." They monitored police scanners all night long, and showed up to cover what the news agencies could not capture with their normal crew. We needed real footage of crime scenes, accidents, and other tragic events that happened while others slept. Doesn't sound very positive, I know, but this was how we set the scene to tell the stories of the real people who arrive at hostage standoffs or run into burning buildings for a living.

One of the best stringers around was Paul Ennis. After several phone conversations explaining our mission of Good News, Paul wanted to meet and talk more. Our first meeting revealed a shared concern about truthful story-telling, making the world a better place, and our common values regarding children and family. I revealed that my husband and I had two sons, the youngest who was born with a birth defect. Paul seemed visibly touched, both by our personal story and by our mission.

"You really need to meet my sister," he blurted. "You and Leslie are two peas in a pod. You will be amazed. You two are so much alike!" Paul went on to say that his sister Leslie and their father, Ed, had put together an amazing organization called A Touch of Understanding. He ran out to his car and returned with a brochure and a business card, encouraging me to call her and talk.

70

I don't remember how long it took for Leslie DeDora and me to meet, but I do know that when we did, it was as if we had been born from the same set of genes. I immediately loved her mission—to create understanding for others with differences. As a former school teacher, she knew that changing the hearts of young people would set the stage for a kinder generation of adults. I knew we would be working together. I knew we would be friends.

Over the years, I've had the absolute pleasure of promoting ATOU personally and professionally. Together, we produced videos to raise both funding and awareness for the organization and a video for the classroom presentations. Television and radio stations offered airtime to interview Leslie and her team. My production team helped build the ATOU website, and I had the honor of serving on the Advisory Board. I began to see young people everywhere with disabilities, and would encourage them to become speakers at ATOU.

Never will I forget the first time I attended a school presentation by this group. Young children changed from being fearful and uncertain about kids with disabilities, to having a healthy curiosity, showing compassion, being kind and welcoming. In an interview after a presentation, a young boy told us that he once teased other kids who could not walk "right" or who learned differently. He told us, "I've changed my mind. I understand now. I'm sorry I was that way. I will never treat other kids like that again." I was moved to tears...so very grateful that this group was committed to changing the hearts of children towards others with disabilities...and at the same time, so very sad that ATOU was not around when my son was small.

However, the added blessing is that our son grew up to

become one of the speakers for ATOU. This was just one more way for him to know how valuable his life is, just as he is. Speakers of ATOU are born ambassadors for good, catalysts for change, and pioneers for acceptance of things we may not otherwise understand. Their lives are critical to a world that needs compassion.

A Touch of Understanding is a group that touches hearts in places others can't seem to reach. Their message is life-changing for some, and a guiding light for others. Their story is the epitome of good news, and I was blessed to have the good fortune to share it with others. Mission accomplished!

"The difference between try and triumph is a little umph."

—*Marvin Phillips*

Melinda Sayers

ATOU Speaker

I was so excited when I learned about ATOU. I thought to myself, "This is where God wanted me to be." I knew that I could reach others, and that is exactly what I am doing.

Melinda Sayers

When I was three years old, my parents and doctors could not figure out why I only weighed seventeen pounds. I ate handfuls of butter and anything else I could get my hands on. Unfortunately, nothing worked. Doctors conducted exploratory surgery, and determined that my bowels shut down. I was diagnosed with pseudo-obstruction of the small bowel, a motility disorder. Digesting food is extremely difficult for me.

The amount of food an average person digests in a few hours may take my body over a day to digest. If I eat, my stomach hurts—the type or quantity of food is irrelevant. It helps if I don't eat every day, but it is difficult not to eat, since our culture revolves around food and meals.

Since I cannot eat, I receive nutrition through intravenous feeding with a catheter that goes through my subclavian vein. I receive a fluid called T.P.N. (Total Parenteral Nutrition), which contains the majority of my nutrition. I could not have made it through my hard times without the help of dedicated family and friends.

My younger sister also has this disability. She, unfortunately, was diagnosed at age of six and therefore has a few more difficulties than I have. Since my sister was malnourished for the first six years of her life, she has a more difficult time learning and communicating with others. However, she is still very smart and will go back to school soon. I also have a younger brother who is as healthy as can be. No one else in the family has had this disability. Through all of my hardships, I am still grateful. I know that there are people who are worse off than me, so in a way I am thankful. I would be a totally different person without my disability.

"You have choice. You can select joy over despair, happiness over tears, action over apathy and growth over stagnation. You can select you ~ and you can select life."

—*Buscaglia*

Tukey Seagraves

ATOU Speaker

I Choose Joy

It has been my observation that all too often we look at what is happening around us—and to us— and think that life is just dealing us one bad hand after another. It is so easy to get caught up in the negative that we sometimes forget there is also positive light that shines through that darkness, lighting the way.

Tukey Seagraves

It was July of 1988, that my husband Dave and I sat in the doctor's office and listened as he explained how all the tests I had undergone indicated that I had multiple sclerosis (MS). I wasn't sure at that point exactly what that would mean, but I was sure it wasn't good. From the time we left the doctor's office, until hours after we arrived back home, I was in tears. "This just couldn't be happening to me. Not now." The more I read about multiple sclerosis, the more frightened I became. There are a lot of symptoms associated with MS, but my fear seemed to focus on the possibility of losing the use of my legs.

My life had been one filled with blessings. I have a wonderful husband, two beautiful children, a spacious home, terrific friends, and an inner life that seemed to be growing by leaps and bounds. I was happy. I was excited about what might be waiting ahead of me. However, in the weeks following my diagnosis, I spent a lot of time in tears, looking at where I had been and where I was headed. I had felt the breeze on my face as I flew through the sky with the wonder of a baby bird on its first flight, wondering where this new experience would lead me. "This couldn't be happening to me. Why would God teach me to fly and then clip my wings?" My fear was turning into anger. I really became caught up in the "what ifs" and the depression was hard not only on me, but on my family as well.

It didn't happen at a certain time, or in a certain place, but over time. I began to see that the negativity that I was allowing to control my life was not how I wanted to live the rest of my life. My life was still filled with meaning and purpose. I still had the love and support of a wonderful family and caring friends. I had always been a positive person. What was happening was blocking the light of that positivity.

My husband and I attended a marriage workshop where we were taught that "Love is a decision." This was something I had struggled with until I experienced it for myself. I remember thinking one morning, as I sat at the breakfast table, feeling hurt at the angry words I had exchanged with my husband. All of a sudden it occurred to me to think about what was happening. I could either sit all day and brood over what was a silly little argument and have a horrible day, or I could decide that I was going to just love him in spite of it. I had a choice: I chose to love, and my heart and my day were both lightened.

I am sure that this was the basis for my being able to come to grips with the diagnosis of MS. I came to see that joy is also a decision. I could choose to be happy. But, I found that deciding to be happy isn't a one-time event. I have long periods of good times when I don't think about the MS. But I also have bad days when I have to choose several times in one day that I am not going to let the depression, that comes so easily, control my life.

One particular event stands out in my mind. One morning, as I was getting out of bed, I noticed my right leg would not lift off the floor. Two days later the left leg also became affected. My worst fears seemed to be coming true. It was a hard few months. But with the help of my family, my friends, a very positive neurologist, and mega doses of prednisone, I regained the use of my legs.

In fact, six months later, my husband and I made a very strenuous hike to the top of Half Dome in Yosemite National Park. A lot of people have accomplished this feat but to me there was an extra sense of accomplishment. I had not only overcome my worst fears of having MS, but I had experienced one of the highest points of my life sitting on top of that mountain and gazing down into the beautiful Yosemite Valley. Having MS made the feeling of reaching the top of Half Dome even greater and more powerful.

About five years ago, I became involved in A Touch of Understanding. It is always such a joy to share my story with the students who come to hear about what it is like living with disabilities. I have received such love and support from them. I remember one young man who told me his mom had MS. To be able to share how I was able to deal with my MS helped him see that his mom could do the same. ATOU is all about joy in the midst of living with a disability of any kind.

I love reading Victor Frankl's book *Man's Search for Meaning*. This man endured years of unspeakable horror in the Nazi death camps. He was an internationally renowned psychiatrist who came from a wealthy family. Through this atrocious experience, he lost everything he held dear. But listen carefully to his words.

"The experiences of camp life shows that man does have a choice of action.... Man can preserve a vestige of spiritual freedom, of independence of mind, even in such terrible conditions of psychic and physical stress.... Everything can be taken from a man but one thing: the last of the human freedoms— to choose one's attitude in any given set of circumstances, to choose one's own way." I choose joy.

"Now and then it is good to pause in our pursuit of happiness and just be happy."

—*Guillaume Apollinaire*

Jenny Zimmer

ATOU Speaker

I was born with cerebral palsy. Despite my disability, I have thrived in many aspects of my life. I prefer to focus my energy on my talents, and it has served me marvelously thus far.

Jenny Zimmer

Since sixth grade, I have participated in a variety of sports activities, including snow and water skiing, track and field, and wheelchair basketball. I have also received many athletic honors. In 2005, I was one of only thirty-six USA athletes selected to participate in the Australian Junior Games. I traveled with Wheelchair Sports USA as part of Team USA for Track and

Field, returning home with two gold medals from the event, in shot put and discus.

I also like to give back to the community and teach others through my experiences. I greatly enjoy serving as a counselor-in-training at Wave Camp, a summer camp for children with physical disabilities. As a former Wave Camper, I have found another way to give back to the community that allows me to thrive. I have also volunteered with Project Play and Ability First.

In addition to my athletic and community service accomplishments, I am pursuing a therapeutic recreation degree at Sacramento State University. My positive experiences through adaptive sports have motivated me to give back my knowledge and experiences to others with disabilities. In the future, I hope to work for Disabled Sports USA or Access Leisure, nonprofit organizations that support individuals with disabilities.

ATOU caught my attention through a Sac State Therapeutic Recreation class. I appreciate the unique experiences and education provided through this organization, and became a speaker for the program. I end every presentation with the statement, "The wheelchair is part of me, but not all of me."

In addition to speaking, I developed an annual ATOU event called Dreams to Goals. I created this program so that children know that dreams can come true, and that nothing is impossible. The day is centered on kids reaching their dreams. Each year, the day-long workshop has a theme, such as "Ingredients for a Dream" or "Building Blocks." Each child is paired with a mentor, someone who is charged with helping the child to figure out what he or she is good at. The child has the opportunity to listen to the mentor who, in turn, provides motivation and direction. After this workshop, the children should have motivation to achieve their goals. We have had many success stories, including one person who went to film school because of this workshop. It has been a very successful event.

Family Connections

"It is only with the heart that one can see rightly; what is essential is invisible to the eye."

—Antoine de Saint-Exupery

Hope Adrian

ATOU Speaker and Member of the ATOU Youth F.O.R.C.E.

The wonderful thing about kids is that they're naturally inquisitive. They want to explore the world around them, but that inquis-

Hope Adrian

itiveness can quickly turn to discomfort and awkwardness if their questions aren't answered. When it comes to disability, people, whether that be kids or adults, often don't get their questions answered, so when they run across people with disabilities, as they inevitably will (school, work, community), they don't know how to handle themselves. As unfortunate as it is, their discomfort, more often than not, results in avoidance of the person they view as different. As a person with a disability myself, I can tell you that this scenario plays out often, and it can be very isolating, especially growing up. When people see me in my wheelchair they stare, or worse, avert their eyes. They don't say "hi" or introduce themselves; they just walk away or whisper to their friends.

A Touch of Understanding is a game-changer. It allows kids to get their curiosity satisfied and become comfortable with what was previously a scary situation. More importantly, it breaks down social barriers by answering all their questions and, as a result, awkwardness is resolved and the kids are finally able to see that people with disabilities are just people—that we like playing sports, video games, watching movies and monkeying around on the playground just like them.

When I started volunteering with ATOU at ten years old, I had no idea what I was doing or the impact we were making, but I now know that we are changing the perception of disabilities, one school at a time.

That's when the magic happens. The kids finally start making connections—making friends. Bullies are turned into buddies, and apprehension is turned into acceptance.

"When you look at your life, the greatest happiness's are family happiness's."

—Joyce Brothers

Ginger Adrian

Parent of ATOU Speaker and ATOU Youth F.O.R.C.E. Member

It's a beautiful thing...to see your ten-year-old daughter being treated like a rock star at school, rather than the "invisible" girl in the wheelchair. She was treated like a rock star because she found the courage to share her story with her schoolmates to help them understand what it's like to live with a disability. She talked about how her classmates are all more similar than they are different, and how her likes and dislikes were much like

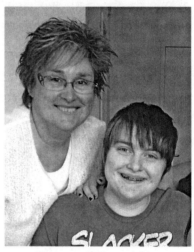

Ginger and Hope Adrian

their own. She concludes her presentation with, "Look to your left. Does that person look like you? (Heads shake no.) Look to your right. Does that person look like you? (Heads shake no.) Could that person be your friend? (Heads shake yes.) So, even though I look different, could I be your friend?"

With her service dog by her side, she blossomed as she continued to share her story with ATOU as a guest speaker at elementary schools, Sacramento State University, and various civic organizations. Her ability to inspire others and her sincere desire to help make a difference in the lives of people with special needs drove her to suggest that perhaps ATOU might get more kids involved with the program. As a result, ATOU Youth F.O.R.C.E. (Friends Offering Respect, Creating Empowerment) was created. ATOU Youth F.O.R.C.E. is a place where kids with and without disabilities interact together and within the community. The program is a place to meet new friends, share adventures, contribute through community service and try new things–a place to belong.

I'm so very thankful for ATOU in our lives. Hope's involvement with her ATOU family has given her the opportunity to become the confident, caring, and compassionate young woman she is. As she heads to college in the fall, her strength of character, leadership skills, determination, and ability to respectfully advocate for herself will take her a long way. Thank you, ATOU, for giving her a place to shine.

"Accept the challenges so that you can feel the exhilaration of victory." —*George S. Patton*

Stephen Christian

ATOU Speaker and Member of the ATOU Youth F.O.R.C.E.

Stephen Christian

A Touch of Understanding has meant the world to me in more ways than people will ever know. The best moment I ever had was when ATOU recognized my birthday. I was pretty down, but my dad told me about an event held by ATOU, and he convinced me to go. When I got there, everyone was excited to see me. Stephanie said that ATOU had a birthday gift for me. I was expecting a card or something small. They had a box of books, candy, a card deck, and a game.

I know it doesn't sound like much but those few items meant the world to me.

Life is 10 percent what happens to you, and 90 percent how you react to it."

—*Charles R. Swindoll*

Andre Christian

Parent of ATOU Speaker and ATOU Youth F.O.R.C.E. Member

Andre Christian

The very first time we heard about A Touch of Understanding our son Stephen participated in a workshop at his elementary school. He was so excited to see a group that was for people who had special needs like him. Over the years, ATOU has become an extended part of our family. ATOU is an inclusive group that has many activities that directly and positively help children develop into confident, loving, and well-adjusted young adults. We are so grateful for the positive influence that ATOU has had on our family. When I think of ATOU, the quote from Margaret Mead comes to mind. "Never doubt that a small group of thoughtful committed citizens can change the world; indeed, it's the only thing that ever has." Without a doubt, A Touch of Understanding makes a positive difference in our community, and ATOU makes this world a better place.

"To live is the rarest thing in the world. Most people exist, that is all."
—*Oscar Wilde*

Kiersten Schmidt

ATOU Speaker and Member of the ATOU Youth F.O.R.C.E.

Kiersten Schmidt

I am twenty-four years old and was diagnosed with autism at the age of four. I certainly had no idea at four years old that I had autism, but I definitely knew very early on that I was different than the other kids, especially since I had two sisters very close to my age. I went to a special preschool focused on language for two years, since I barely spoke. After that, I was placed in a special day class that was also for children with significant language delays for the next three years. This class was at a different school than where my sisters went, and I remember having to take a special bus to get there and we didn't really get a chance to interact with any of the other kids at the school. What I really wanted was to go to the same school that my sisters and the neighbor kids went to. After third grade, my mom petitioned for me to go to my local school. It took over a year for me to finally be accepted and, while that was what I wanted, it was a very challenging transition because I really wasn't accepted by my classmates. For the next three years, I struggled trying to make friends and just trying to fit in, and I started to become very depressed and sad most of the time.

I remember coming home from school in fourth and fifth grades and spending hours on my floor just crying and wishing God had never given me this thing called autism that made everything in my life so challenging. All I knew was that I didn't have any friends, academics were challenging, and I didn't have the skills or coordination to be on any sports teams. Luckily, I had a great family, two amazing sisters, and a church youth group, but I longed for a friend and to no longer feel like an outcast.

My life took a huge change for the better when ATOU came to my class in the sixth grade. They presented their program, and I will never forget how the kids reacted. They immediately started being nicer to me, included me during recess activities, and even invited me to their birthday parties. It was like I had all new classmates, and I was finally starting to make friends. Honestly, I don't think I realized how much the ATOU presentation affected my classmates. One thing that still stands out to me was how a girl in my class, who was really sweet, and also a leader in the school, took the time to ask me questions about my disability and made an effort to get to know me. When everyone saw how kind she was to me and how she made an effort to be my friend, it seemed like others followed in her footsteps. This truly was the beginning of many positive changes as a result of ATOU.

What I remember most about that presentation was that one of the speakers (Mike Penketh)* had a service dog named Magy. He shared how his dog was his best friend, and how he couldn't imagine his life without Magy. I took one of the bookmarks he passed out from an organization called Canine Companions for Independence (CCI). I couldn't wait to go home after school and show my mom the bookmark to see if there was any way I could get one of those dogs, too.

*Mike Penketh, see page 34

My mom said she would look into it, but my grandma was dying at the time, and I knew my mom was really overwhelmed, so I put the bookmark under my pillow and I prayed every night that I could get a dog like Magy. I finally have a best friend, too. My grandma passed away a couple of months later, and my mom called CCI to start the process of getting me my very own service dog. It took about fifteen months, but the timing was perfect. I had to go to a new school, and I was back in a special day class again where I didn't know anyone, so having a dog made my life much better.

Starting high school was very scary, and I was extremely nervous about going. Luckily, most of the kids had been in the school district since grade school so they heard the ATOU presentation. My high school experience was so much better than I ever hoped for, and I know for sure it is because of the ATOU program. First of all, I was reunited with all the kids from my sixth grade class who saw the ATOU presentation. Secondly, thanks to ATOU, I had a service dog at school with me, and a dog in a blue and yellow vest is like a magnet to teenagers. Everyone wanted to know why I had the service dog, which allowed me to tell them about my autism and explain how the dog helped me. They found it very interesting. I was even asked to speak in my choir class and tell them about why I had a service dog and help them understand what autism was. Within days, the school newspaper got word about my presentation to my choir class and wanted to do a story about me. Once that school newspaper was released in the fall of my freshman year, I felt like the most popular kid on campus, and the students truly made a huge effort to say "hi" and include me in class activities. This also had a trickle effect on all the kids in my special day class, and I believe it made it a much better place for them, too.

I volunteered with ATOU through high school and helped them implement the autism component of their program. After I graduated from high school, I became one of ATOU's regular speakers. I love being a part of this amazing organization that has changed my life in more ways than I could have imagined. First and foremost, they made my school years much better by helping my peers have a better understanding about disabilities. Secondly, they introduced me to CCI, and having a service dog for the past twelve years has been one of my greatest blessings. I cannot imagine my life without a dog by my side.

ATOU has helped me to become a public speaker, which has opened many other doors for speaking opportunities. I have become more confident, and I am no longer ashamed of having a disability; in fact, I look at it as an opportunity to show people that in spite of having autism, I too can have a fulfilled life. I love sharing with people everywhere I go that I am a public speaker for a disability awareness organization and sharing what we do during our presentations. People are always so supportive, and I know in my heart that I, too, am making a difference.

In addition, I have had the privilege of working with some of the most amazing people who have hearts bigger than I could have ever imagined. The ATOU family that I am a part of is made up of people with and without disabilities, and each one of them wakes up every morning with the same goal in life and that is, "To change the world we live in and make it a better place for people living with a disability by educating people one presentation at a time." I have found friendships at ATOU that I know will last a lifetime, and I am so proud, thankful, and blessed to be a part of such a wonderful organization. I look forward to being involved with ATOU for many years, and only hope I can give back to them just a portion of what they have given me.

♥

"If a man empties his purse into his head, no man can take it away from him. An investment in knowledge always pays the best interest."
—*Benjamin Franklin*

Charity Schmidt

Mother of ATOU Speaker and ATOU Youth F.O.R.C.E. Member

I am the mother of three beautiful daughters, Kiersten twenty-

Charity Schmidt

four, Rachel twenty-two, and Rebecca twenty-one. I was so excited to be blessed with three children and never gave any thought to one of them being born with a disability. However, when Kiersten, our oldest daughter, was just turning one, it started to become obvious that she wasn't reaching all of her developmental milestones, and I was becoming concerned.

Her pediatrician wasn't concerned at all, but my motherly instincts told me that something was wrong; and as it turned out, I was right. That was the beginning of our days being filled with doctor and therapy appointments, and our quest to find out exactly what was going on with our beautiful firstborn child. Kiersten was finally diagnosed, just after her fourth birthday, with Pervasive Developmental Disorder or PDD, which is on the autism spectrum. While we were happy to finally have a diagnosis, we were challenged with the question, "What do we do now?"

We had two younger children and were overwhelmed with all the information we were reading on autism, the different intervention options, and what the future holds for people with this diagnosis. Kiersten was placed in a special day preschool that focused on language, since she was pretty much nonverbal at that point. She spent the next two years there, and then transitioned to another Special Day class (SDC) for first- through third-grade students with significant developmental delays in language. She went to SDC for another three years, but started asking to go to school with her sisters. She was starting to realize that she was different than her sisters and their friends, because up until this point, all she knew were students similar to her.

We petitioned our school district to allow Kiersten to be mainstreamed at our local grade school, but they were extremely reluctant and that process took well over a year. Surprisingly, the teachers were not very familiar with autism and were not sure how to accommodate her in the classroom. She went to Resource for most of her academics and stayed with her peers for the remainder of classroom activities.

Academics were only a portion of her struggle. I think her social struggles were an even a bigger issue, because the students did not really understand why Kiersten was different, why she talked to herself a lot, or why she rocked her head so much. These behaviors isolated her, and at this point, she was old enough to see that she was not being included, and that she was never invited to any school activities. This left Kiersten very sad and oftentimes crying and wishing she didn't have autism.

As she would often say, "I hate my life, and I wish God didn't give me this dumb disability. Why couldn't He make me like my two sisters?" Obviously, as a mom, I was devastated and my heart broke for her. I did everything possible to arrange play dates for her and hosted lots of social activities at our house in an effort to help Kiersten make friends. However, as Kiersten got older my efforts weren't working any longer, because the kids were getting older and making their own social arrangements.

Kiersten was starting to become very depressed and spent a lot of time crying, mostly just wishing she could be included and have friends like her sisters did. At home, it was much easier because her sisters always included her, but at school, they didn't have the same lunch and were in different grades.

It was the fall of Kiersten's sixth grade year when ATOU came to her classroom and did a workshop. I will never forget that day, because when I picked her up from school she was beaming from ear to ear and so excited to tell me all about her day. She showed me the book she had received from ATOU, told me all about the workshop, and could not wait to show me the bookmark that she had gotten from the man who had a service dog there to help him. Probably what Kiersten remembered most, was the man telling the class how his service dog, named Magy, was his best friend and how she did everything with him. For Kiersten, a service dog was the answer to her sadness and no friends. All she could focus on was how she, too, wanted a dog to have as a best friend.

It was early fall, and my mom was battling terminal cancer and nearing the end of her journey. While I was happy to see Kiersten so excited, I was overwhelmed with emotions and what the next couple months had in store for us. Kiersten asked every day if she could get a service dog like the man from ATOU, but honestly I didn't have the energy or the time to look into it. I promised her I would do it later, but I was focusing on caring for my mom. Every night I saw Kiersten staring at that bookmark and saying her prayers and asking God to help her get a service dog. She then would place the bookmark under her pillow and go to sleep night after night, never giving up on her dream of a dog. My mom passed away in early November and after the funeral was over and we were getting our lives back together, she asked again. I called Canine Companions for Independence (CCI) and started the process of getting Kiersten signed up for a service dog. Thirteen months later, Kiersten received a beautiful yellow Labrador named Horace.

Horace changed Kiersten's life in more ways than we could have ever imagined. She was in seventh grade now and in another full day SDC classroom, but every day, Horace and I would pick Kiersten up from school and it was like they were wearing a magnet. The kids waited in line to pet Horace and Kiersten was now meeting so many kids, she couldn't possibly keep track. When she got home from school every day, she'd lay on her bed with the biggest smile and would spend hours talking with him and loving on him. They literally did everything together and as Kiersten would say: "I never care about not being invited to sleepovers because I have a sleepover with my best friend every night of my life."

Her prayers every night were thanking God for her new dog and best friend, and thanking Mike* from ATOU for sharing his story of having a service dog. Kiersten stayed involved with ATOU all through high school and they often asked her to speak at some of their special events, especially when they were speaking about autism or to high school students. It wasn't long before local newspapers started doing articles on Kiersten and her dog, and soon she was being asked to speak to local autism organizations and at CCI fundraisers to share her story about how having a service dog changed her life. Within just months, Kiersten was speaking on a regular basis, and even her

*Mike Penketh, see page 34

doctors could not believe her progress or the difference in her; they had never witnessed such growth in a patient with autism like Kiersten.

I can say, without hesitation, that A Touch of Understanding changed Kiersten's life the day they came and did a workshop in her sixth grade class. It drastically changed how the students treated her, and I am confident it is because they finally started to understand why Kiersten was different. ATOU's message helped peers to embrace her differences, instead of shying away because they didn't understand her. After their workshop, Kiersten started being included at lunch, she was invited to parties, and she felt more accepted by her peers. In addition, we would have never known about the possibility of having a service dog for Kiersten if it were not for Mike's presentation about how his service dog has supported him both physically and emotionally.

I am confident that having a service dog for the past twelve years has helped Kiersten become the confident speaker and young adult she is today. She has been a speaker at ATOU workshops for the past five years, since graduating from high school, and she thoroughly enjoys every minute she gets to spend with this amazing group of people. They have nurtured her, encouraged her, loved her, and helped her blossom into the beautiful and confident young woman she is today. I have had the blessing of watching each and every ATOU person pour their heart and soul into the hundreds of volunteers who support this incredible organization and the work that they do.

As a mother of a child with a disability, ATOU has definitely been the answer to so many of my prayers. No mother could ever imagine how an organization of people could love their child as much as I know so many people at ATOU love mine.

While all of Kiersten's friends at ATOU may not be her age, she has been blessed with some incredible lifelong friends that I know she treasures with all of her heart. I am overwhelmed by the gratitude of this organization and its volunteers who just keep on giving. I hope that one day I have the ability to give back to ATOU as much as they have given to Kiersten and our entire family. We are so very grateful for their generosity and their mission to change the world we live in—one workshop and child at a time.

"When we are no longer able to change a situation, we are challenged to change ourselves."

—Victor Frankl

Paige Whitefield

ATOU Speaker and Member of the ATOU Youth F.O.R.C.E.

I was born three months too soon, weighing one pound, twelve ounces. My parents were told that I had suffered a severe stroke on both sides of my brain during birth, due to my premature birth. If by some miracle I would survive, they were told I would never walk or talk.

Paige Whitefield

During my first two weeks of life, my parents were unaware of my head swelling and were shocked and surprised to find that I was scheduled for surgery to treat my progressing hydrocephalus. Hydrocephalus is when excess fluid of the brain does not drain properly. A shunt was placed to drain this fluid. Since then, I have had four surgeries and have gone thirteen years without having another shunt operation.

94

I am proud to say that I have proved the doctors wrong. In 2006, I was fourteen years old and, by the grace of God, a fully-functioning person with only right-sided hemiplegia. Hemiplegia is a condition which affects the right or left side of the body, causing the muscles to stay in constant contraction. Due to this condition, everyday obstacles are endless, but I have found ways to overcome them.

Amazingly, I have learned to ride a bike, which most kids with hemiplegia never dream of accomplishing. I have also performed in twenty-eight musicals. Most recently, I have joined the team of A Touch of Understanding, which has become an activity I am most passionate about.

Being a speaker for A Touch of Understanding gives me a chance to be in front of an audience, which I love. Telling my story reminds me of all the things I've overcome, which gives me joy and more confidence. I think the students like the fact that I'm close to their age. I am able to help them understand what life is like for me every day. I tell them it's hard enough to have a disability, but when kids tease you, it makes it much more difficult.

A Touch of Understanding is important because it communicates that people with disabilities are normal people. We like to laugh and watch movies. These kids may have a disability themselves one day, and if that happens, they can look back on their experiences with A Touch of Understanding and remember that we are content and happy with our lives. And they can be, too!

"The best and most beautiful things in the world cannot be seen or even touched—they must be felt with the heart."

—*Helen Keller*

Susan Whitefield

Mother of ATOU Speaker and ATOU Youth F.O.R.C.E. Member

Susan, Paige, and Monte

I am the mother of Paige Whitefield, a wonderful young woman who has been shaped by her amazing opportunities in life. As a tiny preemie at 1 pound 12 ounces, developing hydrocephalus and cerebral palsy, and undergoing eight surgeries (to date), she has had enthusiasm to persevere and overcome her challenges.

Paige's love is theater, and she started performing at the age of seven. She loved being on stage in front of an audience. By the age of fourteen, she had participated in over thirty musicals. She also chose to become a cheerleader for girls with disabilities, and cheered at disabled sporting events. When Paige heard about A Touch of Understanding, she decided she wanted to get involved. It seemed like a perfect match for her: speaking to groups of children about her life and being center stage. As her mother, I was excited for her to be an active participant in the program. Since Paige was homeschooled, this was a great opportunity with her flexible school schedule.

Paige seemed to have natural talent in public speaking. She learned her speech and looked forward to sharing her story with the kids. Since Paige was one of the first children to be a speaker with ATOU, she was involved with every adult who volunteered.

I knew Paige loved speaking, and I knew she would be a great influence on the children who heard her story. What I failed to expect, was what a great influence all the amazing volunteers would have on Paige's life, and mine.

My involvement was driving Paige to events and being her support. Since Paige has grown up in physical, occupational, speech, and vision therapies, we have been exposed to people with many disabilities. Being around the ATOU volunteers, I became friends with people with disabilities which I had not been exposed to. I have to say, honestly, that at first, I was uncomfortable. Here I was, a mother to a physically disabled child, yet I was uncomfortable around people with disabilities. It gave me firsthand experience of how others might feel around my own daughter.

It was through contact and friendship that made me feel totally at ease. This was an eye-opening experience for me. It made me realize what a service ATOU does for everyone, but especially children, so they can learn to be comfortable with those who are different at an early age. This is a valuable and necessary lesson.

When I observed Paige speak to the children, I saw what an impact she made on them. I could see that they felt like she was a friend, a classmate, just like them, but looked a bit different. I watched and listened to their questions for her, and watched her confidence build in the process. I could see that she felt important, valued, and special. I could see the kids swarm around her after her presentation to ask more questions and just be closer to her. She felt like a star, and they seemed to be star-struck getting to know someone different. They learned that she was just another child, like themselves.

Paige also grew in her friendship with the volunteers. I would say that this was the only place she felt totally accepted for who she was. She was truly loved by all these wonderful people, and she loved them, too. She really grew up at ATOU with the influence of adults who cared for her, nurtured, and accepted her. Her confidence continued to grow.

ATOU is an organization that promotes acceptance through education and experiences with people. I believe it has amazing benefits to all of those involved, not just the children who learn from the program, but also the volunteers who work together, even for a mom just driving her daughter to events.

Unfortunately, school became more time-consuming, and Paige's volunteering ended. I do believe her experience with ATOU shaped the person she has become. And, in just a couple of years, she plans to be back working with school children as a speech and language pathology assistant. She will still be working with kids, and is still interested in speaking/language. To ATOU and all the people there who have influenced her life and mine, I thank you!

Support System

"Start by doing what's necessary, then do what's possible, and suddenly you are doing the impossible."

—*St. Francis of Assisi*

George Arrant

ATOU Workshop Activity Instructor

My journey to become a volunteer began long before the existence of ATOU or ADA rules. In 1962, at the age of twelve, my sister Carol was stricken with spinal carcinoma. The ravages of this disease required radical surgery, which left her so that she no longer could walk. My memories of her are of a vivacious and interesting person. Her courageous spirit, her love for other persons, her concern for education, her appreciation of the good, and her youthful insight into spiritual things, made you want to grow inwardly.

My mother provided the nursing and nurturing care Carol needed. She continued her studies at home with the help of the home teaching program, and received a diploma with her graduating

George Arrant's sister Carol

class of McClatchy High School. For this accomplishment, she received many letters of congratulations, including a letter from then-Governor Ronald Reagan.

She successfully developed handiwork skills, such as knitting, artwork, and Plexiglas casting. Some of her handmade articles were made as gifts she gave to her friends. About four years prior to her passing at the age of twenty-eight, her physical condition worsened, and she could no longer use her hands.

My most vivid memories are of comfortable summer nights when she would sit outside in the front of the house with her cocker spaniel Blondie and the neighbor, talking about the day's events. Also, the two trips she made to Disneyland were highlights in her life.

In late December of 2011, I received a phone call from a friend and fellow ATOU volunteer Mike Penketh* wondering if I would be interested in attending an ATOU workshop. Since I was retiring, I said "yes." A few years earlier, I had attended an ATOU event so I had a pretty good idea what it was all about. Once there, I knew this organization was the right fit for me. Many of the traits that I previously described about my sister, I

*Mike Penketh, see page 34

found in the wonderful volunteers that I worked alongside. It is as if I have come full circle in this journey.

"Unity is strength... when there is teamwork and collaboration, wonderful things can be achieved."

—Mattie Stepanek

Dave Delgardo
ATOU Volunteer

In the 1950s, I grew up with a mother who was born and raised in Texas. In the South in her day, there were certain things one thought about certain people. American Indians wore war paint. Black people needed to know their place. "Cripples?"— that was mom's word—cripples were people who we were supposed to fear and pity.

Dave Delgardo

In my first grade class, a boy named Mike had been born without a right arm. Down the street lived another boy named Bruce who was "mentally retarded" and went to a special room at school. Across the creek lived a girl known as Bunny, who lived in abject poverty and always smelled kind of funny. Around the dinner table, each was spoken about in hushed tones and with downcast eyes. Frequently used was the word "pity." My brother and I were advised that we probably shouldn't play with these classmates for reasons I didn't then understand. Irrationally, I figured I might catch what one of 'em had. I knew Mom didn't want that for me.

101

When a classmate named Danny barely survived a fire while riding in his dad's camper on the way home from the World's Fair in 1962, we had another poor kid to pity. When Bruce's mom, Donna, was diagnosed with cancer, another name was added. More downcast eyes. More hushed commentary. More fear.

FAST-FORWARD TWENTY-FIVE YEARS. I was a fledgling principal shepherding children at a tiny, newly built public school in the Sierra foothills. Important to us would be community. Our credo would be that we cared for one another. We would be a great big family, and I would be the dad.

Yet, when a blind girl named Chelsea enrolled, the first thing that came to my mind was pity. And when Timmy came aboard needing specialized toileting care, fear incubated. Finally, when a boy known as DJ enrolled with his disruptive, repetitive behaviors (we knew little of autism at the time), I felt the little community I'd tried to build was on the verge of collapse.

My sincere and talented staff ruminated greatly. We may or may not have had the heart, but we certainly lacked the strategies to fully embrace these unique and beautiful—yes, beautiful—special learners. Can't we send them someplace else? I left that school with my few defeats outweighing my many victories.

When I opened a school in Granite Bay, I found myself with a staff just as talented as those with whom I'd worked in the hills, serving a population not dissimilar to my former community. The principal difference was that I could find fear and pity only in myself.

In January of that first year, I found out why. A van pulled up to campus and out of it poured a mix of cheerful individuals excited about spending a morning on my campus. They brought with them activities involving mirrors, canes, guide dogs, prosthetic arms, and wheelchairs. They demonstrated that they could move from place to place in spite of paralysis. They could see in spite of being blind. They could communicate like us, tell amazing stories like us, laugh like us, and even fly airplanes—which most of us couldn't do. In fact, nothing seemed out of their reach.

The students were amazed. They explored using the devices and wheeled themselves around in chairs. They learned what it was like to have their brain process things backwards. And they tumbled over themselves asking questions of our guests. No question was off limits, no answer evasive. The teachers took all of this as simply another day at school. Why? Because A Touch of Understanding had been to their school before—many times. Ingrained in staff was the knowledge that all students are simply students, each has potential, and none brings anything to fear.

The morning of their visit, I rediscovered a simple truth or two: The precursor to fear is often ignorance; and the antithesis of pity is potential. A Touch of Understanding, the organization that had lit the way for so many students before I'd arrived, had lit the way for me. All I needed to do was to keep the light burning in myself so I could be the leader—the dad—of the great big family I'd always wanted.

My mom is ninety-three. She is legally blind and depends on a walker. I drive North 75 miles four or five times a month to take her shopping, balance her checkbook, enjoy a meal at the Italian restaurant with her, and talk about the old times and the wonderful opportunities she'd afforded me.

I was going to tell her about A Touch of Understanding. Instead, I've decided to simply live it with her: like the member of a great big family might do.

103

"The most important thing is to enjoy your life—to be happy—it's all that matters."

—*Audrey Hepburn*

John DeLury

Member of the ATOU Board of Directors

John DeLury

I became acquainted with ATOU in 2003, through my association with the PASCO Scientific Foundation. We formed the PASCO foundation that year and committed to hosting a quarterly company meeting with a non-profit guest speaker. The first quarterly meeting included A Touch of Understanding as our invited guest. One of our board members had heard of ATOU and thought it was a perfect connection for our newly formed foundation. I met Leslie DeDora and her father, Ed Ennis, at that meeting. Leslie and Ed addressed the company, telling the ATOU story. They spoke with such clarity and passion that the message was an exceptional success. PASCO has been a solid supporter of ATOU ever since that day.

Personally, I experienced two events in my younger years that put a soft spot in my heart for children with disabilities. At the age of seven, my family was blessed with a baby girl born with severe cerebral palsy. Lynn passed away at age two, but forever left me with empathy and appreciation for all those coping with a disability, and for those unsung heroes who committed to be of service to them and their families.

In college, I was associated with a service club, Circle K, and we sponsored a day school for children with disabilities as our primary community project. So when I heard the ATOU story told so eloquently by Leslie and Ed, it resonated deeply within me and I knew with certainty that I had to get involved. Upon my retirement from PASCO in 2011, I contacted Leslie to explore board membership. I was accepted to the board that year and have been working with the ATOU team at various levels ever since.

The experience has been unbelievably gratifying. Meeting with, playing with, and crying with precious children, their families, the ATOU staff, and numerous selfless volunteers is an incredible experience. ATOU touches so many people, young and old, with a message of compassion, respect, and friendly acknowledgement that it needs to be heard everywhere. That is my belief and, thanks to ATOU, the message is getting broadcast and clearly heard by thousands of people. Lives are being changed every day for the better. It doesn't get better than that. Thank you, ATOU!

"The art of being wise is the art of knowing what to overlook."
—*William James*

David Dominguez

Member of the ATOU Board of Directors

David Dominguez

My experience with A Touch of Understanding goes back to my days as an elementary school principal. I worked in several school districts in Placer County in my career, and I sought out the services of ATOU while working in each district. The reason was quite simple: it is the only presentation that addresses the need to educate students and staff with resources and information about students with disabilities. The workshops are hands-on and presentations are delivered from volunteers who themselves have disabilities.

At first, I thought the workshops were important for students to learn to be sensitive and gain knowledge about students with disabilities. However, the effect it had on teachers and staff was just as powerful in giving them the tools to assist students and feel more comfortable in their approach to transitioning students with special needs. Additionally, the parents of all children felt a sense of relief in being better prepared to be more accepting and understanding of what all children need, especially those who have disabilities.

The ATOU volunteers are incredibly open, allowing students to ask any questions without feeling embarrassed by awkward moments. When I retired, it was a no-brainer to want to support such an amazing non-profit like ATOU. I feel privileged to be a part of such a wonderful organization that makes a positive difference.

"Slight not what's near, while aiming at what's far."

—*Euripides*

Kim Nash

ATOU Workshop Activity Instructor

This is my first year volunteering at the workshops with ATOU, and it has been a rewarding and fun experience every time I step on a school campus. I don't have a disability or any family connection with one, but it touches my heart to get involved with any organization that teaches acceptance. I learned of the organization when my three children were lucky enough to have the experience in elementary school. They are all off to college and beyond now, so it is nice to be able to spread this message that impacted them so many years ago.

Kim Nash and family

The whole world benefits as children grow up with a better perspective and understanding that all people deserve to be appreciated and respected. School-aged children are such a terrific target for this message. They are open to new ideas and genuinely have big hearts. Mostly, they are simply unaware and mystified by the various disabilities we present, so taking away this mystery has a magical effect.

Leslie's opening message to the children is wonderful, and they all seem to come to the stations eager to learn and appreciate what it may feel like to walk in the shoes of someone with a disability. I primarily instruct them in Braille and walking with the white canes. They surprise themselves at what they can learn and experience in the few short minutes we get with them. I never tire of hearing the "wows" when they successfully write their name in Braille, or the exclamations as they struggle with the white canes.

I know children are also strongly impacted by listening to the speakers. I have met many of the speakers and know how fortunate the children are to have them share their stories and life experiences with them. It is such a unique opportunity to bring this message into the classroom, and it is fun to talk to the children at the stations after they have heard the speakers. Students each get something different from the experience, but it is always interesting to hear their perspectives.

It is my pleasure to be able to be a small part of delivering this message. The world is clearly a better place because of the dedication of Leslie DeDora and her community of volunteers.

"Education is…hanging around until you've caught on."

—*Robert Frost*

Bob Schultz

Member of the ATOU Board of Directors

Reducing bullying and making every child feel safe and valued was a key goal in my classroom over sixteen years as a teacher, in my school in six years as a site administrator, and in my district in ten years as a curriculum leader, and four years as a district superintendent.

Bob Schultz

I was often in charge of finding programs to help my schools combat bullying and create a safer learning environment. To be honest, the best ones had only a short-term impact and were soon forgotten, while the others had no impact at all. A month after a program had come through I could find no evidence of positive change at my schools.

Then, in 1998, I came to Eureka Union School District and was encouraged by a retired friend to come and see a program for which she volunteered at Greenhills School. By the time I navigated around the school in a wheelchair, walked with my eyes closed using a white cane, tried to trace a racetrack by looking in a mirror, wrote my name in Braille, and learned something about invisible learning disabilities, I was hooked. After going through the stations, I went into a classroom and heard a handful of amazing adults and young people share their stories and describe how they had overcome a potentially disabling condition or incident and could focus on what they could do instead of what they couldn't.

By the end of the workshop, I was in tears, and in awe, of the way every student tuned in to the presentations, and not a moment was lost in a very full half-day workshop. Founder, Leslie DeDora, a tiny paid staff, and an army of volunteers had provided the best program I had ever encountered.

Curious to see what the students had to say after the program, I went into classrooms and found rich conversations going on, as students admitted that they had been afraid of some people with disabilities, or had said cruel things to other students in the past, but they weren't going to do it again. They generalized from the specific disabilities they encountered in the ATOU workshops to the ways that any one of them might feel different or shut out by others. The kids got it!

When I talked to teachers and administrators weeks after a workshop, I heard that the program's impact was still visible long after the group had departed. In the years ahead, several parents talked with me about how their child with autism, their child in a wheelchair, or their child who had to walk with braces went all the way through our district without ever being bullied or ridiculed, or made to feel less important than anyone else. That is success.

When I retired as a school superintendent, every non-profit I had ever heard of was ready to fill up my "free-time" by me helping with their meaningful organization. However, I knew where I wanted to be, and I was honored to join the ATOU Board of Directors. Every time I attend a school workshop, a Youth F.O.R.C.E. activity, or any project put on by ATOU, I am reminded again of why I serve. Put simply: A Touch of Understanding changes lives for the better.

Youth F.O.R.C.E.

Friends Offering Respect ~ Creating Empowerment

"Everyone thinks of changing the world, but no one thinks of changing himself."

—*Leo Tolstoy*

Robin Boparai

Member of the ATOU Youth F.O.R.C.E. and Granite Bay High School ATOU Youth F.O.R.C.E. Club

Working with A Touch of Understanding has been a life-changing experience. The work that this wonderful organization does to educate students about disabilities has truly made a difference in our schools and communities. They have touched so many lives and demonstrated the importance of understanding. As a volunteer with ATOU, I have witnessed the change that the organization has made. I have seen the effects of their work in my own school. As a result of ATOU disability awareness programs, students are more willing to reach out to individuals who are bullied or excluded due to their differences.

111

ATOU has taught me a great deal about some of the challenges experienced by individuals with disabilities. The Youth F.O.R.C.E. has shown me that anybody can make a difference simply by offering support and companionship. Working with ATOU to alleviate some of the hardships faced and to provide support has been an unforgettable experience. I have learned so much from the resilience and strength of the students with whom I have worked. These students have overcome the hardships of their disabilities, whether physical or intellectual.

Robin Boparai

ATOU has proven the importance of a positive outlook, support, and strength in overcoming adversity. Seeing a beautiful smile on each student's face when I attend ATOU events brightens my day and demonstrates the impact of the organization's work. I am so grateful to work with ATOU to help spread acceptance and understanding.

"Accept the challenges so that you can feel the exhilaration of victory."

—George S. Patton

Ryan MacIntosh

Member of the ATOU Youth F.O.R.C.E. and Campus Leader for the Granite Bay High School ATOU Youth F.O.R.C.E. Club

"Hi Ryan!" Although I hear these words on campus on a regular basis, they made more of an impact on me when Matthew, a special needs student at my school, greeted me. I realized I made an impact on his life, and on the lives of many others. I would have never heard him say those words if I hadn't challenged myself.

Ryan MacIntosh (center) at an ATOU Youth F.O.R.C.E. event

During my sophomore year, I volunteered to help at a Valentine's Day party put on by ATOU. ATOU is an organization that helps raise awareness about intellectual and physical disabilities. All I knew going into the night was that I would be paired up with someone with an intellectual disability. My partner was a girl named Taylor, and throughout the night she told me all about herself. Before going to the event, I researched the effects that an intellectual disability has on someone's personality. My research taught me that many special needs people don't like being touched; they are cautious of others encroaching on their comfortable space. At the end of our night

113

together, Taylor wrapped her arms around me and thanked me for being her friend. That hug gave me feelings that I wanted to relive over and over, because her joy made me feel so good.

I immediately joined the ATOU Youth F.O.R.C.E. Club at my school. I attended meetings and more events, similar to the Valentine's Day party, where I got to see Taylor again. Leading into my junior year of high school, I wanted to be more involved with the club, and I was selected to be on the ATOU Youth F.O.R.C.E. Club Board of Directors as Campus Leader. As the campus leader, I designed weekly lunchtime events where students came into a classroom and interacted and played games with the special needs students. My goal was to combine general education students and the special education students in an exciting atmosphere. I wanted to make general education students more aware of intellectual disabilities, while at the same time, making the special education students feel comfortable around other people and allow them to make friendships that they would otherwise not have made.

When Matthew greeted me that day, I realized I accomplished my goal because I made him feel comfortable and provided him with friendship. Making positive impacts is a passion of mine. When I am passionate about something, I am determined to not let any adversity stop me. I work hard in all aspects of my life. I am advanced in both academics and athletics because I am passionate to do well. Helping others achieve happiness is another passion of mine. I am eager to attend college and look forward to furthering my goals by applying what I will learn with passion.

"I can't change the direction of the wind, but I can adjust my sails to always reach my destination."

—Jimmy Dean

Amberlynn McLoed

ATOU Speaker and Member of the ATOU Youth F.O.R.C.E.

I am twenty-one years old and I have a physical disability called cerebral palsy. In spite of my disability, I love to snow and water ski.

When I was thirteen years old, I was very depressed and I came home from school every day, crying, wondering "Why me? Why do I have a disability?" My mom was worried because I would say, "You don't know what it is like to have a disability." I felt alone and out of place.

Amberlynn McLoed

In 2010, my friend Jenny Zimmer* started the "Dreams to Goals Workshop" at A Touch of Understanding. That is where my ATOU career officially began. One of my favorite moments was the first time I spoke at an ATOU event, because I was fulfilling one of my dreams. Speaking was something I wanted to do since I first heard about ATOU. I started to be a speaker at workshops, and I love to be a speaker for ATOU! I got asked to be a speaker at the "15 Year-50,000 Students Celebration." I will never forget that night because after I got done with my speech, there wasn't anyone who wasn't crying in that room.

ATOU and the Youth F.O.R.C.E. have changed my life in many ways. ATOU helps me to reach my goal of becoming a

*Jenny Zimmer, see page 77

115

motivational speaker. I get to meet people who want to change peoples' perspectives about the disabled community. At a Youth F.O.R.C.E. activity, I met a boy who is also part of ATOU's Youth F.O.R.C.E. I asked him if he would like to come to my junior prom with me, and he said "Yes!" So, I had a date to my junior prom! Now I have a date for "Night to Shine"—the same boy who took me to my prom five years ago.

ATOU is the most important thing to me. I'm not sure how I would have gotten out of my dark stage without ATOU. ATOU has helped me feel that I can make a difference in the world. I know ATOU has made a difference in my world and has been a positive influence to many others, as well.

"Children are our most valuable resource."

—*Herbert Hoover*

Vyas Srinivasan

Member of the ATOU Youth F.O.R.C.E. and President's Assistant and Education Secretary for the Granite Bay High School ATOU Youth F.O.R.C.E. Club

I came to know A Touch of Understanding because ATOU came to our elementary school when I was in third and fifth grades. We got to use wheelchairs, read Braille, etc. I started getting involved with ATOU in 2015. I wanted to start a club at Granite Bay High School (GBHS) that taught social skills. I used to go to a social skills group on Saturdays, and I got inspired by the group's lessons.

Vyas Srinivasan

When I tried to start my club at GBHS, I had some issues. I asked the speech therapist and the school psychologist to be the advisors for my club, and they said they couldn't do it because they were advising the ATOU Youth F.O.R.C.E. Club. The day I wanted my club to meet conflicted with the ATOU club, and it was also held in the same classroom where I wanted my club to meet. A teacher mentioned that my club and ATOU had similar goals and that we should merge. The first ATOU event I attended was the Roseville Holiday Parade, and I really enjoyed it. Additionally, I made more friends by teaching in the GBHS Youth F.O.R.C.E. Club. Being part of ATOU helped me to learn about different disabilities, and it has given me opportunities to hang out with my friends outside of school.

"There is always one moment in childhood when the door opens and lets the future in."

—Graham Greene

Sara-Kate Pirnik

President of the ATOU Youth F.O.R.C.E. and Youth
Representative on the ATOU Board of Directors

When I was in the first grade, I had a very difficult time understanding my Aunt Sara's disability. She has autism and I did not understand why she acted differently from other adults I knew. After A Touch of Understanding visited my school, I finally began to understand what disabilities were and that I needed to be a friend to all of the disabled people I met.

Sara-Kate Pirnik

This experience with ATOU has stuck with me, which is why I was so excited when ATOU came to my school when I was in the sixth grade. After this visit, I became obsessed with the idea of volunteering for ATOU because I really supported their message. Two years later, I began to volunteer for the ATOU Youth F.O.R.C.E., and I fell in love with it!

The Youth F.O.R.C.E. meets once a month to plan monthly social events for people of all abilities. I began to volunteer more and more with the Youth F.O.R.C.E. and, at the end of the school year in 2014, I was asked to be the president. Having the Youth F.O.R.C.E. be such a big part of my life for the past few years has been truly life-changing, and I would not trade all of the new friends I have made for the world.

Sara-Kate is the President of ATOU Youth F.O.R.C.E., and is a non-voting representative on the Board of Directors.

"When you are kind to others, it not only changes you, it changes the world."

—Rabi Harold Kushner

Anjali Suthahar

Member of the ATOU Youth F.O.R.C.E.

Anjali Suthahar

"Everybody is a genius. But if you judge a fish on its ability to climb a tree, it will live its entire life believing that it is stupid," said Albert Einstein. Everyone has different and unique abilities, and people should respect those abilities, not judge based on appearance or actions. Before I was introduced to A Touch of Understanding, this quote wouldn't have

118

made sense to me. I used to be scared and uncomfortable around people with disabilities, and didn't understand their disabilities. I remember, the first time my mom brought me to an ATOU event, I was still unsure of what it was. ATOU teaches children about disabilities, and gives them an opportunity to "walk a mile" in the shoes of someone who has a disability. When I heard this, my first reaction was to be nervous. I was afraid that I would say something wrong, or do something I wasn't supposed to do, and hurt someone's feelings.

The first person I met was Mike* and his dog Magy. I hadn't realized that Mike had prosthetic arms, and I proudly showed him how flexible my thumb was. To my utmost astonishment, Mike showed me how he could turn his arms 360 degrees! From that moment on, I was drawn to ATOU. My perspective on disabilities changed, and I now understand more about different abilities, which has helped me befriend many people with disabilities.

One of the main reasons that ATOU has changed my thoughts about people with disabilities is because I've been lucky enough to meet many people who have disabilities. These people have made me realize that people with disabilities are just like everyone else, and they want to be treated like everyone else.

One person that truly inspired me was a man named Byron**. Byron is a major Disney fan, and goes around in a cool wheelchair with his cowboy hat and boots. When Byron had a surgery several years ago, the doctor's needle accidently poked his spinal cord, and made one of his legs hypersensitive and the other completely numb. It was so interesting to hear Byron's experiences during the school workshops. Once, someone he knew spoke to him very loudly, thinking that since he was in a wheelchair, he must be deaf as well. This made me realize that

*Mike Penketh, see page 34
**Byron Chapman, see page 148

a lot of people aren't educated about different disabilities and are unaware of what people with disabilities can and can't do. Because people are unaware, they become afraid.

Meeting Hanah*, a 14-year-old girl who adores acting, also changed what I thought of people with disabilities. Hanah is on the autism spectrum. As I befriended her, I was truly inspired. Hanah memorizes plays, embracing certain character roles whole-heartedly. She is a very playful and caring person.

After meeting Byron, Hanah, and many other people with disabilities, I've realized that compared to people at ATOU who speak about their disabilities (and many others), I haven't experienced many hardships at all. For example, I don't really like to interact with people whom I don't know, but some of my friends at ATOU are able to bravely and humorously speak about their disabilities. I really respect them, because they have faced so much, yet they don't let their disabilities hold them back, and that shows true courage. These inspiring individuals have motivated me to always persevere, even when my task is difficult.

Another element of ATOU that molded my perspective of people with disabilities is the Youth F.O.R.C.E. The Youth F.O.R.C.E. is a part of ATOU that provides fun activities and events for people with and without disabilities to mingle. I've helped plan some events, and have been able to work with people with disabilities as a team. At a planning meeting, I teamed up with a girl named Courtney to make a flyer. Courtney** is a beautiful, blond-haired teenager who is very sweet and kind. I was intrigued by her dream to be one of the princesses at a Disney park. She is paralyzed on one side of her body. At first, I thought that I would offer to do the typing, but Courtney was able to type pretty easily. I underestimated her when I thought Courtney would have had a lot of trouble typing. Even though this

*Hanah Stover, see page 144
**Courtney Osiow, see page 57

incident wasn't overly important, it still impacted me because it shows how much determination people with disabilities can have and what they can accomplish. I've learned through the Youth F.O.R.C.E. that instead of being afraid, I should be a friend to people with and without disabilities.

Once, I went with my mom to one of the ATOU workshops and participated in the different stations. Along with other activities, I was able to experience how people with autism and learning disabilities feel. At the learning disabilities station, I drove a racecar through a maze on paper. Instead of looking at the paper itself, I had to look at a mirror in front of me and draw. It was extremely difficult because everything I drew went backwards, and the exact opposite of what I wanted to do.

This made me understand how frustrated people who have learning disabilities can feel sometimes. I learned that the reason people with learning disabilities have trouble reading and writing is because their minds switch letters and numbers around, making it harder to read and write. The entire workshop really taught me to be kind to everyone, no matter how they look or act. I learned many other values, such as perseverance, patience, and compassion. The workshop changed how I thought about people with disabilities, because now, I knew more about different disabilities.

Meeting people who work at ATOU also altered my thoughts about people with disabilities. Leslie DeDora, the founder of ATOU, inspired me greatly. She is such a caring person, and comforts everyone around her. Susie Glover[*] is another thoughtful individual, and she is always genuine and sincere. Jackie Callahan[**], a fun and bubbly lady, always keeps the mood bright and cheerful. All my friends at ATOU are hard-working, and never give up when they are completing a task. They have

[*]Susie Glover, see page 135
[**]Jackie Callahan, see page 49

taught me a lot about kindness, and how we should be caring and understanding towards everyone, no matter what they look like.

All of my experiences at ATOU have changed my perspective about people who have disabilities, and have made me a better person. The values I've learned can be applied not only to people with disabilities, but to the greater world. It is important to be kind and compassionate towards everyone, including people who are discriminated against and judged, not just people with disabilities. ATOU has helped me understand much about the world and myself, and has helped me be nicer to all.

"Attitude is a little thing that makes a big difference."

—Winston Churchill

Anna von Wendorff

President of the ATOU Youth F.O.R.C.E., Youth Representative on the ATOU Board of Directors and Founder of the Granite Bay High School ATOU Youth F.O.R.C.E. Club

When I think of how ATOU has impacted my life, my first thought is "confidence." I volunteered with ATOU for more than three years, often coming in several times a week. I served as president of the Youth F.O.R.C.E. and, later, worked with the Board of Directors as the first youth representative. I still consider myself very much a part of the ATOU family, but due to distance (I am currently a student at Stanford University), I am now limited to watching the events from afar.

Anna von Wendorff

The first time I met the people who make up some of our ATOU family was

122

at the Kiwanis Easter Egg Hunt at Cavitt Jr. High School. I was a newly minted high school freshman, heavily involved in Key Club (a community service club sponsored by the Kiwanis), and extremely shy. The Kiwanis Club had invited several organizations—among them, ATOU—to set up booths near the entrance. Despite having never seen a workshop (my school started workshops after I graduated—not fair!), I heard about this organization that taught and practiced disability awareness and kindness. For two hours, I eyed the ATOU table, staffed by Leslie and Susie*. I was too nervous to approach a table of strangers and ask questions about an organization I only barely knew. I did a (kind of) sneaky walk-by, and I think Susie saw right through me. She smiled and invited me over. Relieved, I accepted and heard about all of the programs offered by ATOU. I left with all of the flyers and papers I could find on the table.

It was not until Susie sent me an email the following day, along the lines of: "it was great to meet you; why don't you stop by our Youth F.O.R.C.E. meeting next week?" that I decided to actively go to these events. So, with gentle pushing and prodding on behalf of ATOU, I was able to step out of my shell a little bit.

I remember sitting around the table in the office at my first Youth F.O.R.C.E. meeting, a collection of young people whom l had never met. The first person who introduced me to the wonderful participants in ATOU was this incredible young woman named Hope**. Hope was sitting at the table, knitting, casually calling out ideas and suggestions, and throwing in Harry Potter and Doctor Who references for good measure. She was so confident, eager, and excited that it made me want to join this group more than ever.

After this, I went to just about every event. I took on more of a leadership role each time. One of my favorite events the first

*Susie Glover, see page 135
**Hope Adrian, see page 80

year was the first annual Valentine's Dance. I came early with the other Youth F.O.R.C.E. members to help decorate, then spent most of the time chatting with people on the outside of the dance floor, silently amazed at the confidence that so many young people had to get up and dance in the middle of the floor, in front of so many people. No matter if they had a wheelchair, crutches, or earpieces, they came to dance, and no one and nothing was going to stop them. I remained rooted on the outskirts of the dance floor, absolutely positive that I wasn't going to get out on that floor and dance in front of so many people. Think of all of the embarrassing things that could go wrong: I could forget a dance move, run into someone, fall over.

Flash forward one year. At the Second Annual Valentine's Dance, you could find me at the microphone calling out songs, at the snack table, or at the sign-in table. But still, I stayed a safe distance from the dance floor. I wasn't sure anyone wanted to see me dance, and I was still sure I would be silly and embarrassing.

One more year thereafter, at the Third Annual Valentine's Dance, one of the younger Youth F.O.R.C.E. members grabbed my hand and literally tugged me onto the dance floor. And I danced! I had so much fun jumping around to the music, spinning around, bumping into people on accident, and lip syncing (the completely wrong lyrics). I realized then that the point is to be silly and funny and happy. That is the biggest "skill" that I learned during the two years in which I acted as Youth F.O.R.C.E. president. I was able to mentor youth who met for our Core Group, who planned events and made decisions they would otherwise not have been delegated.

My experience at ATOU taught me how important it is to act as a mentor, something that I continue to do at Stanford. I have discovered mentors at ATOU who inspire me every day to work hard and to do "good" no matter where I go. I also began to understand the basics of event management: how to brainstorm, plan, spread the word, and finally, lead the event. I am eternally grateful for these connections, skills, and friendships I gained from ATOU.

After acting as president for a number of years, I was invited to join the ATOU Board of Directors as a youth representative. I was welcomed by a wonderful, talented, and caring group of individuals. I learned so much about the financials behind a non-profit, as well as the legal structures and difficult decisions that must be made. Having this opportunity at such a young age is unusual: I am able to take classes at Stanford's Graduate School of Business, present valid reasoning, and offer real-life examples. I feel comfortable in these professional settings as a result of my time spent on the Board of Directors. I learned about the wide and complex world of "social change" with a remarkably skilled, influential, and kind group, who had the patience to listen to and accept my questions and ideas.

The wonderful people I met at ATOU—from the staff, to the volunteers, to the youth—have pushed me to become sillier, friendlier, and more confident. I have gained skills that I would otherwise have never learned: how to manage events, fundraise, and apply for grants. I don't think of my time at ATOU as volunteering, because I got so much more from ATOU than I could ever give. More than anything else, I am glad that the students who have taught me all of this have a safe and open environment to build upon their strengths, and I value the mentorships and friendships that I have found along the way. ATOU is a place where each of us is both a student and a teacher every day. I feel lucky to have fallen in love with such a meaningful and powerful organization, filled with such inspiring teachers and students.

Past and Present Staff Members

"Memories of our lives, of our works and our deeds will continue in others."

—Rosa Parks

Meghan Adamski

Youth F.O.R.C.E. Coordinator, Assistant to the Executive Director

Disabilities have always been a part of my heart. In elementary school, my best friend had cerebral palsy. In high school, my best friend Dara had muscular dystrophy. Unfortunately, I have lost touch with my elementary school best friend, but Dara continues to be a huge part of my life and was a bridesmaid in my wedding. She used her chair, and was no different than any of the other bridesmaids.

Meghan Adamski

I got my degree from Sacramento State University in speech pathology, and through college, I found myself continually in jobs that worked with children, primarily with autism. I did in-

126

home therapy, worked at an after-school program for children on the spectrum, and then worked as a speech pathology assistant at a clinic that primarily served children on the autism spectrum. I enjoyed what I did, but I had an epiphany and realized that my real calling was to educate others about disabilities.

ATOU came into my life about seven years ago but, at that time, I had no idea where it would lead me. I had a friend who was doing her internship with ATOU, and she needed some extra hands at a dinner fundraiser. When I had this epiphany in the spring/summer of 2014, the name "A Touch of Understanding" kept coming to my mind because of that one event so many years ago. I took it as a sign that I had to reach out. The first time I called, I talked to Jeneane*, and within a matter of a few minutes, I knew that my heart found what it was looking for. I knew I had to be part of this great agency. A couple weeks later, I found myself in the office speaking with Leslie, Doug**, and Susie***. "WOW" was all I could say. I felt at home. A couple of months after that, I was at a gathering, and when driving home, I called my mom, and with the biggest smile on my face, I said, "These are my people." I knew that ATOU was exactly what I had been searching for in life, and so much more.

Since immersing myself in this world, I have gained a family. I have made lasting friendships in such a short amount of time. I have been amazed by strength and, at times, have been pushed to find my own. I have found a constant source of support and encouragement. I have found a life-changing group of people that embody everything I want to see in this crazy world. Recently, at dinner with a friend, I was listening to her talk about sadness and lack of hope in the world. I listened to

*Jeneane Stover, see page 144
**Doug Newton, see page 140
***Susie Glover, see page 135

her and thought of all of the joy and hope that surrounds ATOU every single day. I shared some stories, and within minutes, a smile swept across her face, and she said "You're right, there's so much joy and hope in this world."

"You'll learn more about the road by traveling it than consulting all the maps in the world."

—Unknown

Kody Fernandez

ATOU Workshop Activity Instructor, Volunteer Coordinator, Member of the ATOU Board of Directors

It was fall semester 2011, at Sacramento State, in my last class of the day. I was sitting in the back of the classroom and listening to the guest speakers pitch their agencies to try and get us to volunteer with them. We only had to complete 30 hours in 16 weeks. I had already decided I was going to work with "old people or kids," and no one in between.

Kody and Joyce

The first speaker was someone from a senior citizens center in Rancho Cordova. I thought, "How convenient, old people will be my choice." Then, another woman was talking about some program they do with kids. I didn't even catch the name of the organization. My mind was already made up: I would complete my hours with old people.

Then another young woman came into the classroom in a wheelchair. Her name was Hope*. Hope has cerebral palsy. She introduced herself and began talking about cerebral palsy and

*Hope Adrian, see page 80

128

service dogs. She couldn't have been older than thirteen, and she had a vast knowledge of service dogs rules and regulations. She also explained Youth F.O.R.C.E., another program offered by the organization. By this time, I was hooked. I looked at the brochure to check out the name, A Touch of Understanding. Within a few days I called Susie, the volunteer coordinator, and set up a time to check out the program. My first program was at a school in Rocklin. I participated in the workshop with the students and was blown away.

After that day, I went to almost every Friday workshop during that semester. I probably completed my thirty hours within the first couple of weeks. I slowly started to feel like I had a new group of friends, and later, a second family. At the end of the semester, I was offered a job as the ATOU volunteer coordinator. This was a new adventure for me. I was also working another job at the time and attending CSU Sacramento full time. The best part of the job was being able to meet new people, new volunteers, and helping them learn how to assist at the different activity stations.

I was able to learn a lot about working at a nonprofit and a lot about myself. A year and a half later, I was offered another job with the state, which I took, but I later came back and completed an internship with ATOU. I still volunteer with them, and I am now on the ATOU Board of Directors. I love everyone there: staff, volunteers, and animals. I really don't consider my time with ATOU as getting in my volunteer hours. I look at it as hanging out with friends and family.

"The outside of a horse is good for the inside of a man (and a woman)."

—*Winston Churchill*

Pamela P. Gehrts

ATOU Speaker, Grant Researcher/Writer

In 1990, I developed early-onset Parkinson's disease at age thirty-five. At the time, I was home-schooling my two small children, both under the age of seven. In 1980, I earned my master's degree in urban and regional planning, and for the next ten years, I worked hard to build up my consulting business, which was thriving. I was determined not to let this "foreign invader" take me down. However, the harder I fought, the more ground I lost. By 2001, Parkinson's brought me to my knees—literally.

For two years, day and night, I laid on the living room floor. My weight dropped to 130 pounds and my tall 5'9" frame was gaunt and weak. A trip to the restroom required me to crawl on all fours, down a long hallway, to the toilet and return to my "living room place" in the same manner. The pain in my legs was unbelievable and my whole body regularly shook with tremors. I was

Pamela P. Gehrts

130

lucky to get one to two hours of sleep per night. I am not proud to say it, but I came to a point where it seemed that life was not worth living. Needless to say, my children, who were both very young, suffered the loss of their mother and were thrust into the daily Hell that Parkinson's brought into our lives.

In 2003, I had a life-changing medical procedure called DBS (Deep Brain Stimulation) that was approved by the FDA to treat Parkinson's disease symptoms, although not to stop the progression of the disease. The procedure was new and not without risks, including stroke, intracranial bleeding, and in rare cases, death. After thirteen years of dealing with Parkinson's disease's horrendous symptoms, I was at a point in the disease's progression that I was willing to take a chance. I could possibly get some relief from the painful leg spasms, balance issues, and dyskinesias (involuntary movements caused by the Parkinson's medication).

Almost immediately, once the DBS was turned on, the tremors stopped, and the majority of the other Parkinson's symptoms—especially the leg spasms—ceased. The eleven-hour brain surgery involved drilling two holes in the top of my skull and the insertion of long electrodes deep into my brain—all of these actions were expertly performed by UC San Francisco neurosurgeon, Dr. Philip Starr, while I was awake. It is necessary for the patient to be awake so the surgeon can ensure the electrodes reach the desired target, the Substantia Nigra (STN). The STN is the main producer of Dopamine, the brain neurotransmitter that allows us to move, think, and feel emotion. The neurosurgeon also checks the precise position of the electrodes to make sure they have not intruded into sensitive parts of the brain—such as the speech, vision, or movement centers.

In 2004, I joined A Touch of Understanding. Here, I was never judged and there was always a hug when I needed one. The staff and volunteers are a combination of people whom have disabilities and those who do not. The main thing that impresses me about ATOU staff and volunteers is their dedication to the program and the kindness and respect that they extend to the volunteers, teachers, and students. I believe this positive behavior is a reflection of ATOU's Founder and Executive Director Leslie DeDora's leadership skills and her desire to have all individuals treated with respect, kindness, and understanding. Most of the three–hour workshops are held three days a week and require volunteers and staff to meet at the ATOU office/carpool site at "O-dark thirty" (sometimes as early as 5:15 a.m.). From there, we travel to the school, unpack the equipment trailer, which consists of eighteen wheelchairs, Braille equipment, orthotics and prosthetics, audio-visual equipment, and much more. At the end of the day, we are tired but we're filled with the satisfaction that we have shared ATOU's message of understanding to the workshops' students.

ATOU has given me a new purpose in my life. As an ATOU workshop speaker, my main message to the kids is that, "I may look different on the outside and sound different, but on the inside I'm just like you." It is amazing to see the changes in the students' faces the longer I speak to them and share my story. The students' looks of bewilderment and cast-down eyes change to looks of curiosity and understanding. When I was really sick with Parkinson's before my DBS surgery, I made a promise to myself that if I ever could move and speak again, I would devote my life to ensuring that people with disabilities are heard and that our voices would make a difference. ATOU and its wonderful volunteer program have given me this opportunity.

In 2007, I became a part-time ATOU employee. My official title is Grant Researcher/Writer. I am so thankful that ATOU gave me the opportunity to fulfill my purpose to serve people with disabilities. My ATOU position was similar to my previous urban planning position in which I wrote environmental impact reports, general plans, zoning ordinances, and worked with demographics. As a planner, I did extensive research and writing, and ATOU uses me in this same capacity—which I love—because ATOU benefits from something I'm skilled at. Locating grant opportunities and writing grant proposals is important because 25 percent of our budget is composed of grant revenues. Finally, it is important to note, that due to ATOU's small size, none of the employees have just one job. We do it all: from vacuuming the office, to cleaning the restroom, to transporting volunteers to workshops.

What a powerful feeling it is to make a difference. As an ATOU workshop speaker, I feel that if I can help change one child's attitude about people with disabilities, then I have achieved my goal for that day. The following is part of my story that I share with the students:

Rusty was a throw-away pet. My friend, Helene, answered a newspaper ad for a horse. She went to view the horse but another horse caught her eye. Over in the corner, stood a forlorn-looking creature, knee deep in manure and lice in his mane and tail. The most obvious thing was the sad look of hopelessness on his face. All of these factors could not diminish his beautiful, kind eyes. My friend asked the stable owner, "What's the story on that horse?" The stable owner replied, "Oh you don't want that horse. His owner skipped out on his board, and I'm not sure what I'm going to do with him." My friend paid the board bill, took Rusty home, and nursed him back to health. Due to a divorce, Helene had to sell Rusty one year later. Her misfortune was my good luck and the beginning of a relationship between a horse and a human based on trust, loyalty, and love.

For the next six years, my disease progressed and Rusty adjusted his movement to my increasing inability to move. Sometimes, when I lead Rusty to his stall for his evening meal, my body freezes and Rusty waits patiently until I can walk again. When I gallop Rusty though a meadow or open field, my body feels normal and free—as if I do not have Parkinson's disease. It is truly a wonderful feeling. Rusty is here with me and on tough days, his loyal and devoted spirit calms me. And of course, Rusty's beautiful, kind eyes remind me that I'm loved—unconditionally. Rusty teaches me many life lessons. Most importantly, he has taught me that animals are wonderful healers and that we should never give up on hope. At age twenty-seven, Rusty is a wise old soul.

The students love to hear about Rusty, and my dog, Sage. By letting them into my life and sharing the things I love: my pets, my grown children, hiking, and gardening, I become a person to them rather than a stranger with Parkinson's. Once these "walls" come down, the students' hearts soften and they open up to understanding and learning about how I live my life with Parkinson's.

Leslie DeDora and her team of staff and volunteers work tirelessly to pass on the message that ALL people, especially those with disabilities, should be treated with respect and kindness. I am a proud and thankful member of the ATOU family. ATOU has given me a sense of purpose and has been a lifesaver for me.

"Give a little love to a child, and you get a great deal back."

—*John Ruskin*

Susie Glover

Volunteer Coordinator, Executive Assistant, Member of the ATOU Board of Directors

Susie Glover

When I was about five years old, my dad was a foreman at a ranch. One of the workers had a daughter named Gloria. She was probably a year older than me and had the biggest smile you can ever imagine. Gloria didn't speak, and she could not hear. It was known to everyone that Gloria was "deaf and dumb." I was very young and didn't really understand this diagnosis. I just knew that Gloria and I loved animals and playing together. Seldom a day went by that we weren't together. It wasn't long before we could communicate as well as anyone who spoke.

It was during this time when I became very ill. The doctors first told my family I had leukemia. After a long and stressful time for my parents, my condition was finally diagnosed as Hepatitis B. I don't remember a lot about this year in my life. I completely missed kindergarten. I do remember my mom pumping me full of what she called "eggnog" because nothing would stay down. I have memories of sleeping in a red leather chair, and I have memories of Gloria always being with me. It amazed her family how we were able to communicate, and my family was so thankful to her for helping them through a very difficult time.

135

Gloria is the only person I remember on that ranch, and I remember her to this day. I was teased because I had white hair, and she was teased because she couldn't speak. It really confused me why they would say such hurtful things. My mother said to ignore them because they just didn't know any better. It was hard to ignore, but because we had each other, we would just keep playing. I know she couldn't hear them, but I know she could read their faces. I still wonder how people can be so mean. I have often heard Gloria's label throughout my life, and it makes me aware of how some can words hurt, especially when adults say them.

I remember other times during my childhood when my parents would demonstrate caring and acceptance. It could be helping people of color whose car had broken down, bringing home a stranger for dinner when he or she was hitching a ride. I cannot count how many soldiers stationed at Beal AFB whom my dad brought home for a home-cooked meal; many of them came back to go hunting. My parents never met a stranger, and no one ever left our home hungry. Compassion was instilled with me through caring, loving parents. I grew up with family members who had various disabilities, never really thinking that they should be treated any differently. Everyone was included in everything. It baffles me to think why anyone should think someone shouldn't be treated the same.

After I retired from thirty-five years in the Postal Service, I found A Touch of Understanding. I started my own public relations business after my retirement, and I was on the board of directors for the Granite Bay Library. I joined the Rotary Club of Granite Bay and through them, I volunteered to work on a joint fundraiser between the Rotary Club and A Touch of Understanding. During the entire event, I didn't actually know what the group was doing on a daily basis. I just knew these were some of the nicest and most dedicated people I had ever met. It wasn't long before I knew I wanted to learn more about the organization and get to know these people even better.

As I became more involved with ATOU, we tried everything you can imagine to raise funds to keep the program alive. Looking back, we had so many fundraisers. I remember having the beer booth at the Roseville Raceway. It was certainly off of our mission, but there we were, serving beer and spreading the ATOU word to everyone who was able to listen. We had such an amazing group of volunteers, and they made it so much fun. It was a lot of work, but a lot of fun. We did Viva Las Vegas at a senior citizens complex. Again, off the path of the mission, but we had fun and doing things we never would have dreamed of. Looking back, we can get hysterical thinking about all the ways we worked to keep the boat afloat, especially with the bad economy. It was sad to watch so many worthy non-profits go under. Along with some dedicated volunteers and our Board of Directors, we all worked so hard to keep ATOU's trailer on the road.

I witnessed so many life-changing events with ATOU, and every presentation I think something tops off the prior workshops. But if I were to pick one time in which we really saw the difference, it was when we were called to a school where a young man was being teased about having dwarfism. Through this experience, I learned a lot about myself. I had never actually met a person with dwarfism and found myself looking to see if I could see him as well. The first time I saw him, another student was picking him up and throwing him around and around in a circle. It broke my heart.

The next day we actually met this amazing young man, and I had the privilege of hearing him speak to his peers. At the end of the speakers' presentations, they answer questions. One of this young man's peers asked him if he could change the way he was, would he? He took a few minutes to answer and said "No, it makes me who I am." I learned so much from this young man, and he has helped make me who I am.

The ATOU Youth F.O.R.C.E. (Friends Offering Respect Creating Empowerment) was actually born from the trip in which we met this young man. We also met three other phenomenal young ladies with disabilities who also had the courage to speak to their peers and tell them about their lives. To speak in front of your own peers about your life has got to be the most difficult thing I could ever imagine. These young people did it, and two of them (as well as the other young speakers in the program) decided they wanted to get to know ATOU better.

To explain how I feel about the involvement in the Youth F.O.R.C.E. is summed up simply as seeing how our world should be. I love seeing young people of all abilities working and playing together. One of the most memorable times I can remember is at our first actual dance. It took the kids months to plan and everything was absolutely perfect. I remember hearing a squeal and we didn't know if someone was hurt or overwhelmed—it was piercing. What had happened is one of our young ladies had asked one of our young men to her prom, and he said yes. This was the first school dance for both of them, and their parents were thrilled. We received an adorable photo of the two of "our" kids at their first prom. The fact that they both used wheelchairs didn't even matter… the perfect world!

These are the leaders of our future, and helping them find their compassion and acceptance is something that I cannot even begin to explain. They want to make the world a better place for everyone. These young people help in planning events, help setup and cleanup, but what is more important is that they are buddies to our kids with disabilities. It makes me so proud to see young people caring about other people and doing something about it.

I was fortunate to be involved with the ATOU team when we decided to make autism a part of the workshop. Nearly every class at the schools had at least one child with autism, and we wanted to make certain the other students understand a little about it. All of our research, the doctors, and the amazing parents helped us to develop a very understandable component that we are all very proud of. Learning about autism really helped me. I actually thought some of these children were just acting up and the parents needed to take better control of them. My grandson is one of the members of the Youth F.O.R.C.E. Last year a young man in his class who has autism wanted to go to sixth grade camp. Because of our boys accepting him and including him, his family agreed to let him attend. All of the boys had an amazing time. Acceptance!

After the development of this component, I can honestly say I feel more comfortable around people with autism. I have some amazing friends who have autism, and they have taught me so much. Their honesty and compassion is unsurpassed. They are who they are, and they don't worry about what other people think. They don't lie and they don't steal, unless it might be a cookie. My personal belief is they should all be in politics; that would save us all.

To me, A Touch of Understanding is an experience. It moves something inside and opens your eyes to see people in a completely different light. Once you experience the program in its entirety, you can never say unkind things without really thinking about it. It might be a little later, but you really think about the words and how they might have made the person feel. I wish ATOU would have been around when Gloria was a little girl. I am sorry to say our families did not keep in touch over the years. I wish I knew what happened to this beautiful little girl. I have to believe she was able to grow up and fulfill her every dream. I wish I knew her today; she could be a speaker for ATOU.

The people I have met because of ATOU have blessed me beyond belief. These are lifelong friends that I can count on, and I know it. We laugh together and we certainly cry together. ATOU is a bond; everyone wants to make the world kinder, and we are doing something about it… One school at a time, one child at a time. We touch people's hearts; we teach them to be kind.

*Susie retired as an employee from ATOU the summer of 2015. She is now a member of the ATOU Board of Directors and a workshop and office volunteer.

"If a man does not keep pace with his companions, perhaps it is because he hears a different drummer. Let him step to the music which he hears, however measured or far away."

—*Henry David Thoreau*

Douglas Newton

Director of Fund Development

I came to ATOU because I wanted to take on work that more closely corresponded to my personal ideals, to the values that make me feel a sense of balance between my work life and the kind of voice I wish to have in society. The values I start with

Douglas Newton

have to do with respecting all people. That is, not to qualify the word "people" with a nationality, a religion, a race, or any other appellation. I really do mean everybody. Ideally, I would like to place a Mobius strip sculpture, which confuses one "side" with the "other" in concrete and steel at the Kennedy Center, where so many political leaders are trained. On one non-side it would say "us" and on the other non-side "them." The title of the piece: "There is no 'them.'"

When I was in fourth grade, I was one of the two best kickball players in my grammar school, John Muir Elementary. The worst player was an awkward Mexican-American kid with bad teeth, Lito. He wasn't good at kickball, and Lito always got picked last. My parents had raised me to be sympathetic to others, and to be considerate. I really took those lessons to heart. So one day, when I was picking teams, it just got to me that he was always getting picked last. I figured it felt really bad. So I chose Lito for my team to make sure he wasn't the last kid picked. Without really processing what I was doing then until later. I now realize that I had learned an important lesson, which is that winning a kickball game isn't nearly as important as somebody's sense of belonging. This small shift in consciousness—that people mattered more than ephemeral satisfactions, and that our collaborative friendship is more important than competition—is the personal philosophy that eventually led me to ATOU.

I also know what it feels like to be a minority, and the confusion and sense of insecurity that you can feel in that situation. So much of life comes with situational logic. This feeling happened when I first went to Taiwan and didn't speak a lick of Chinese. The willingness of local Taiwanese people to help me understand their culture and way of being inspired me to learn Mandarin. That process of cultural estrangement also helped me to examine the underpinnings of my own culture and way of being, in a way that helped me understand that I could consciously choose how I wanted to live—not according to anyone else's dictates but my own.

This, I thought, defined freedom—and comes with great ownership over your own life choices. Some of the useful questions I had to ask myself (and answer) were so fundamental in this period. Who am I really, and what has shaped who I have become? What are my strengths and weaknesses, and how do I manage them? What are my core talents, and how should I cultivate them? What is the essential contribution I want to make in society? How will I explain the trajectory of my life to my children when they are old enough to understand their father's character? Will they be proud? For a long time I have sought to be secure enough with who I am to distance myself from how others regard me, but I really want my daughters to feel good about who I am, and to embody the richness that a life of service constitutes, so that they can find a balanced footing as generous and loving adults. I want them to choose to be kind.

My freedom in my young-adult years allowed me a platform to navigate an independent and unconventional life. The lessons along the way have led me to cherish the idea that all people deserve to have a voice in society. But I will take that idea further. All people deserve to experience love, empathy, compassion, belonging, and the right to invest themselves in lives according to self-determination. It is a highly personal journey to be true to yourself—one that oddly comes into balance through being true to others. When children respect themselves, they also have the security they need to reach beyond their confusion to embrace how others live and choose to live. This recognition of shared humanity creates a better situation for everyone. For me, this is one definition of what dignity means.

When I saw those kids experiencing ATOU at a Natomas school begin to respect themselves while Leslie introduced the various ways people reach their goals, I knew that ATOU was a rare and beautiful organization. By learning about how people with disabilities make their lives work, kids learn that we all have challenges and talents. It isn't what happens to you that matters, but how you choose to respond. Watching our volunteers introduce various tools, and seeing kids put the pieces together is endlessly inspiring. Much like art, which does not tell you what to think but allows you to explore questions, the workshops ask a river of open-ended questions that pool into the ocean of humanity. I now think of ATOU as a diamond of sorts. Choose any angle to look at this agency and you will find the light shines through, in a way that complements the other facets.

It is my honor and privilege to work as the Director of Fund Development. It is one thing to have a job to pay the bills. It is quite another to work at an agency where the work draws me into it, organically. Waking up on a Monday and wanting to go to work is a great feeling.

When I work with Leslie and the other staff members, we go through our work with a sense of urgency for the mission. We get a lot of work done, but always in a collaborative spirit in which everyone in the office has a chance to contribute. Sometimes a stray dog or hummingbird will come into the office, and we find ourselves seamlessly changing roles to meet that unexpected challenge. That unflappable flexibility makes working in this office a kind of strange adventure, in which no two days are alike. Knowing that everyone is working diligently to make for a more inclusive society makes ATOU a rare and amazing place to work. Given the need to get ATOU into more schools and businesses, we will be working together for a long time on this mission. It's a set of challenges worthy of rising to meet, every day.

"The art of being wise is the art of knowing what to overlook."

—*William James*

Jeneane Stover

Volunteer Coordinator

I have always felt that we have so much more work to do with disability awareness, so I am fortunate to have found this amazing organization. I truly feel as though I am doing my life's work.

I was raised by parents who taught me through example that everyone deserves the same respect, regardless of race, skin color, or disability. This value was instilled in me at a very young age. When I was five, I had a friend who wouldn't speak; we were in kindergarten together and I spoke for her—this was something that I was able to do for her and everybody accepted it. My family moved to Northern California when I was six. My first day at my new school, I noticed a young lady with

Hanah and Jeneane Stover

144

a weight issue who was being teased on the playground. We immediately became friends, and we were friends for many years. (Nobody teased her on my watch!) I was a very shy young lady; however, when it came to people not being treated fairly, I wasn't very shy.

And as I grew up and became a young adult, this compassionate personality trait never changed. I was raised with the knowledge that everyone deserves the same respect, and the golden rule was something I continue to live by to this very day.

I am now in my late forties, the parent of an amazing fifteen-year-old daughter on the autism spectrum, and the wife of a man who was not only injured in an automobile accident, but also has several debilitating conditions—some triggered by the accident and some possibly genetic.

I started working at a very young age, and worked over twenty years in the title and escrow industry. I learned many things during those years: my work ethic, professional office skills, and how to stay calm while handling stressful situations. I had to make some decisions about the affect my career had on my family. Then, my son Zach was fourteen, and Hanah was only seven. I had done well at providing financial support for many years, but it had kept me away from home eight to ten hours a day.

I could not deny any longer that my family needed me home more, especially Hanah. I decided to find a part-time job and we had to change our way of life financially, since things would change without my full-time salary and health benefits. Thankfully, my husband had a good job at the school district in the city we lived in, which allowed me the chance to even consider this option.

We are fortunate to live in the same school district where Leslie began the in-school disability-awareness program many years ago. I can remember my son coming home when he was in fourth grade and telling me how he had experienced ATOU at school. I remember thinking how fortunate we were to be in a school district where the students were learning about disabilities. I had no idea at that time how ATOU would end up changing our lives in so many different ways, forever.

A few years later, Hanah's entire third grade went thru the ATOU workshop at her school. I remember being pleasantly reminded about the program. I was taken back with the thought of every student in her grade having a chance to "Walk a Mile" in the shoes of someone with a disability. I felt very hopeful that this had to make a difference in the way other students and teachers would treat Hanah. We had not had any issues at school with bullying, and now I understood that ATOU could have a lot to do with that.

This was also at time when I was going through the process of learning to accept Hanah's disability, thinking about how it would affect her entire life. I found myself becoming an advocate for her.

Soon after, we started coming to ATOU Youth F.O.R.C.E. events. Hanah was almost ten. Finding social things for her was becoming more difficult. The first time we came to a Youth F.O.R.C.E. event, I was immediately more comfortable than I had ever been in a social environment. This was a group of youth, with and without disabilities, coming together to have fun. The monthly meetings and activities have helped Hanah blossom into the outgoing young lady that we knew she was capable of becoming. Meeting other parents of children with special needs also played a very important role for both my husband and I. I can't imagine Hanah's life without the ATOU Youth F.O.R.C.E. She looks forward every month to the meetings and fun events. It has become a way of life for her. She has many friends from these events who go to her school or are in our community.

Hanah is now almost sixteen years old and a freshman in high school. I started working part time for ATOU almost three years ago. My husband was forced to retire early and go on disability because of his health nearly four years ago. But because I work for an organization that believes in putting family first, I am able to take care of my family's needs and work. But the most important thing is that I am able to make a difference in the world for people like my daughter and husband by helping present the disability-awareness workshop several times a week to school children and adults in the community.

I can't imagine our lives without ATOU. It has affected us in so many different ways. I honestly feel the important work that I am a part of feeds my soul and gives me the strength I need to carry on with all of the responsibilities that I have at home. I have also met so many amazing people at ATOU. I work with an amazing staff and volunteers who have become my friends and support system. ATOU's Founder and Executive Director Leslie DeDora is the most genuine, caring, and thoughtful person whom I know. It's because of her that many people's lives have changed, and I feel that my family is just one example of that.

Moving Us Forward

"A pessimist sees the difficulty in every opportunity; an optimist sees the opportunity in every difficulty."

—*Sir Winston Churchill*

Byron Chapman

ATOU Speaker

Byron Chapman

I was born in Aiken, South Carolina, on October 19, 1952, and came to California when I was five. Fast-forward approximately 39 years to December 5, 1991. I was experiencing severe pain on the left side of my neck. The pain was from three prior surgeries during an eighteen-month period. I was tested to see if I was a candidate for a morphine pump. The tests indicated that the morphine pump would do the job and allow a very small amount of morphine to the nerve that affected the left side of my neck.

148

The entry point for the morphine was on my back near the center of my shoulder blade and approximately three to four inches to the left of my spine.

On December 6, 1991, I went into the hospital for an "in and out" procedure (check-in was at 1 p.m., and I was to be home by 6 p.m. that evening). The plan changed. I was put under a general aesthetic and off to "LA LA Land" until I awoke, and "LA LA Land" had turned into a living nightmare. My life and my family's lives had changed drastically.

During the operation, my spinal cord had been compromised. One of the instruments used by the doctor was a long, narrow metal straw-like tube. This tube was inserted into my back to reach the exact location for the medication to be administered at the nerve ending. The doctor had removed the tube several times to insert it in a different angle. The last insertion of the metal tube was pushed all the way through me (missing my heart by the width of a number 2 pencil lead) and punctured my left lung. As strange as it might sound, thank goodness he did that: my lung went down and my heart went into cardiac arrest. The operation was then put on hold. Had this not happened, more damage could have happened.

They stabilized me and brought me out of my sleep. I had entered a world of pain in many different areas of my body and was not sure what to make of it all. My mind told me that I was having a terrible reaction to one of the medications they gave me to put me asleep for the operation. By that time, I had lost the mobility and use of my left leg. My right leg was on fire and had no motor skills. I never got the morphine pump installed, so I still had (and have) the pain in my neck. Over the next several months, depression set in.

Six months later, I finally realized that this was not a bad hallucination, but real life. So, then the work began. Almost three years later with the help of God, my loving wife (Judi), my two girls (Kelli and Julie), other family members, friends, and medical professionals, I arrived at a place when I realized a miracle had happened.

For approximately two years, I waited for a miracle to happen that would change my life for the better, but the miracle had already happened. I was just too distracted to notice. I never saw the total transformation of my quality of life coming. This only happens to others. While I was looking for it in the North, it came at me from the South. Once I realized this was for real, all I could think about was what I had lost and focused on what I couldn't do. I thought I was on the receiving end of a very sick joke with a bad punch line.

At first, all I did was focus on my problem. I realized later that my family was really going through so much more than I was, and that was my only real regret in this process. I should have seen this from the start and didn't. With the undying commitment from my wife and others, I found the light at the end of the tunnel. It was truly a gift beyond words, and it has stayed with me. I was told that good things landed before me, but there were no shortcuts to speed up the process. The tough days during this timely process didn't just disappear when I started to find happiness. I had to learn to replace the "I can'ts" with "I cans."

Every so often I ask God, "Why me? What have I done to receive such a priceless gift and sent on a fantastic journey?" Also, there are times when I think to myself, "Maybe it isn't what I did to deserve this blessing, maybe it is for what I can and will do every morning when I get up to start on another fantastic voyage."

I realized I was given a once-in-a-lifetime gift. I went from hating my wheelchair to treating it like a wonderful friend who is always at my side (literally all the way around me). Mentally, it is another blessing I never saw coming, but I am really grateful to have it. Like many people, I do enjoy the changes I choose to make each day, and prior to my Worst-Best Day, I didn't find as much joy in the changes that I didn't ask for, or want. However, in the last twenty-plus years, I have found so much more enjoyment from the challenges that have come my way and most often not from my choosing. I look forward to the unscheduled challenges and realize that they are indeed more awesome and so much more rewarding than anything I could select on my own, and I am truly blessed.

When that defining moment happened to me on December 6, 1991, I was thirty-nine years old, with my wife, Judi, and our two daughters Kelli and Julie. I was a customer services supervisor for PG&E in Vacaville. Other than the constant pain in the left side of my neck, if you had asked me how I felt about my life at that point in time, my response would have been, "I am the luckiest guy in the world and life couldn't possibly get any better," and yet it did!

Sometimes when people hear my story they ask me if I was angry with my doctor right after I realized things had drastically changed. I say, "YES!" Most people respond with, "You're a better person than I am; I would hate that doctor for the rest of my life!" My response to them is quite simple and justified.

First, my doctor did not come to work that day with the intent to harm me; the doctor was trying to help make my pain go away, and I trusted him. Like all of us can do, he made a mistake, and I am sure that mistake will stay with him for the rest of his life, but I hope it doesn't. Anger takes a tremendous amount of energy. Once I realized that, I used all of my energy to focus on and be thankful for what I could do. Anger can eat away at a person, and I refused to spend any energy on bad thoughts, and I look forward to every day, positive and refreshed. Mentally, it was one of the best things I ever did for myself and for those around me, because happiness breeds happiness.

There are not enough words I can say to explain the true joy, happiness, and wonderful state of mind that I feel, all because of the Worst-Best Day of my life. I have met so many wonderful people, experienced amazing things, and view life on such a high level. When I look down, I can't see the bottom. It is all good, if not great, stuff. If it were not for that fateful day, I would have missed the opportunity to meet and get to know my friends at ATOU.

It has been several years since I had the opportunity to go through ATOU's workshop, which I refer to as the Fun-Shop. I was instantly hooked and knew I wanted to be a part of this fantastic program made up of wonderful, caring, knowledgeable, and nurturing individuals who pull together to make an awesome team. The team consists of mostly volunteers who have a disability. ATOU spreads the word with workshops that include two parts: the hands-on part, and presentations by individuals with various disabilities. ATOU speakers show how life is for them, and most importantly, that they are all different, and yet the same in so many ways. They try to eliminate fears that a person might have about a person with a disability. ATOU accomplishes this in less than three hours. In the past nineteen years, ATOU has reached more than 80,000 students, and counting.

Just when I think life can't get any better, nor should I have additional opportunities, they keep coming. I continue to ask God, "Why me?" Part of that answer comes to me every morning when I wake up and embrace the wonderful opportunity to participate with ATOU and the wonderful friends that I have at ATOU. Each workshop is exciting and rewarding, and little miracles happen at every event. I am truly blessed; there is no doubt about it! Life is good and will always remain so until the day of my passing, and then I will know the rest of the answer of "Why Me God, Why Me?" and Thank God for ATOU!

I would like to share with you a gift I give to myself every night around bedtime. This started approximately fifteen years ago. I think about everything I did and everyone I met that day from the time I woke up until I go to bed, especially the small things, which often turn out to be the best. When I relive each day, I ask myself two questions about that day. 1. Am I glad I did? 2. Do I wish I had? If I find that I have more "I wish I hads" than "I am glad I dids," then the next day, I do what I can to turn those, "I wish I hads" into "I am glad I dids." Life is good and gets better and better each day!

I dedicate this to my loving and caring wife, Judi, who is my best friend. When it comes time for me to review each day, she is always at the top of my list. When I ask myself and I think of her, the answer is always the same, having her in my life, I am glad I did!

"The perception of beauty is a moral test."

—Henry David Thoreau

Paula Henry-Vias

ATOU Speaker

Thirty years ago, I had a stroke at the young age of twenty-five. My whole left side was paralyzed. With the help of wonderful physical and occupational therapists, I learned how to walk again and regain a little movement in my arm. They also taught me how to do things with one hand, like put on my clothes and how to cook only using one hand. That can sure be tricky!

Paula Henry-Vias and Scott Vias

My doctor thought it would be a good idea for me to learn how to ride a horse to help get my balance back. So I found a place that helps disabled people with "horse therapy." Not only did I get my balance back, but I also got back my self-worth. Five of my riding friends and I were asked to be the first Disabled Color Guard in Fremont, California. We had so much fun riding in parades, holding the flags on opening day for Special Olympics, and other events.

I never regained movement in my left hand, so I have learned to do everything with my right hand. In the kitchen, I have a special cutting board with two nails on it. A potato can be pealed by putting it on the nails to hold it for me. To blow dry my hair, I have a device I stick on my mirror with a big suction cup that holds my blow dryer for me. I also wear a leg brace that helps to support my ankle. I consider myself very "handy-capable." If there is a will, there is a way!

I've raised three children and volunteered at their school in the library. For a few years, I worked as an in-home health aide for the elderly. I was an active member of the Pleasant Valley Grange and served on their board for three years. My favorite job is pet and house sitting.

In 2009, I started volunteering with A Touch of Understanding. I am so excited to see how this program has changed the way children think about anyone they perceive as being different. This program will definitely help stop bullying in schools. I am proud to belong to ATOU, because I know it is making a big difference in the way children interact with their classmates and people with disabilities.

"In the depth of winter, I finally learned that within me there lay an invincible summer."

—*Albert Camus*

Doris Hernández-Morales

ATOU Speaker

I am very grateful for being a volunteer at A Touch of Understanding. ATOU shares awareness and empathy for disability. And I, Doris Hernández-Morales, am a stroke survivor. This is my venue and my true heart that I love.

Prior to my stroke, I had a wonderful life with great family and friends. As a first-generation in my family, I received my bachelor's degree at the University of California, Davis, and my master's degree at the California State University, Hayward (now East Bay). When I was a student at UC Davis, I went home

155

Doris Hernández-Morales

very often. I met Martin, who became one of my best friends, and a few years later, we got married. Everything was great.

Then on January 18, 2002, I woke up at 1 a.m. with a bad headache. I called the advice nurse and she told me that I had a migraine. At the time, I was approximately five months pregnant. Because I was pregnant, I did not want to take any medication for the headache. I went back to sleep until 6 a.m., and I felt a little better. I decided to go to work, to do last minute preparations for students who were starting the spring semester. The nurse and Martin insisted that I should not drive to work and asked if I could call someone for a ride. I called Rick, a colleague and a very good friend of mine, and he drove me to work.

Around 11 a.m., I was in my office getting ready to call someone, and I could not see for two seconds. I called my husband to come pick me up. I called the advice nurse and was told that a migraine can last a whole day. When we got home, Martin went to get an ice pack and I went to the bathroom before I was going to take a nap. I had my first stroke at 1 p.m. I tried to get up from the toilet, and I fell down. I called Martin, but all I said was, "Aaaahhhh." He picked me up and took me to bed, and then he called 911, at 1:05 p.m. I had a second stroke at 1:15 p.m., and from then on I don't remember what happened.

I arrived at the hospital and a neurologist immediately did a MRI and diagnosed me with symptoms of a stroke, but could not see anything obvious. The neurologist then conducted a CAT scan and noticed a blood vessel on the backside of my brain was leaking. The neurosurgeon performed the first surgery to stop the blood vessel from leaking. Unfortunately, after the first surgery, the doctor noticed that the blood vessel was still leaking and had to perform a second surgery. During the second surgery, the doctor removed a piece of my skull to relieve pressure in my brain. The piece of my skull was placed in the freezer for a few months at the hospital. A few minutes later, the blood vessel stopped bleeding. Thank you to the wonderful doctors!

I was in the ICU and unconscious for three weeks. Afterwards, I heard everything and everyone, but I could not speak (aphasia). I also had paralysis on my right side (hemiplegia), which I still have. I was released from the hospital in early March 2002. On April 22, 2002, Emilio was born. He is a true miracle. As a mommy, I figured out how to do everything with one hand.

At the end of May 2002, my neurologist put the piece of my skull back in my head. I have a scar, which I truly love, because I'm still here. In October 2002, the neurologist did the Gamma Knife Radiation procedure to fuse the blood vessel. That was the last surgery I had...Yeah!

Speech and physical therapy were incredibly good. We tried so many things, but I could not speak. In 2005, I was able to say a few words and walked very little with a cane. I was blessed that I was able to do even just a little bit. In the end of 2006, I woke up one morning and was just looking at my husband. A few minutes later, Martin woke up, and for the first time, I said, "Hi Baby!" I started crying with happiness. It was only fragments, but I was excited. In 2007, I was able to begin sentences. It was an angel who helped me...I truly believe that.

Today, I have paralysis on my right side. I use a brace that goes from my right foot to the top of my leg, and a brace on my right hand. I can walk (like a turtle) with my cane, and I use my wheelchair to travel distances and at night. Although I am different on the outside, I remain the same person on the inside. I have regained about 90 percent of my speech in English, and 60 percent of my speech in Spanish. I use to be fluent before I had my stroke, but I will keep trying. I think that is pretty good, for not being able to say anything for so many years.

In 2009, I made an appointment with my neurologist. Something was different. They checked everything, and I was fine, but he told me that I was pregnant. Martin and my doctor were excited, yet I was nervous. On April 9, 2010, Noah was born. He is truly a gift from God. I am a true stroke survivor as a wife, a mom, a friend, a family member, and a volunteer. I can do everything, just with my left hand and my left leg. I do it a little differently, but I can do everything. It is actually amazing.

As a stroke survivor, I volunteer, which I love. I started the Stroke Survivor Support Group a few years ago; I also am a member of the Traumatic and Acquired Brain Injury Support Group (TABIS) at American River College; and I am a member of the County of Sacramento Disability Advisory Commission Housing Subcommittee. I truly love everything, but I wanted something else.

In June 2011, Emilio's teacher mentioned that the third grade students would attend an ATOU workshop at Gold River Discovery Center. She invited me to hear about their program, and I did. Once I was there, I was hooked. Everything that I heard was exactly what I wanted to do. I am now a volunteer at ATOU where we talk about disabilities. I enjoy talking to students about my disability, and they love seeing me tie my shoes with one hand. I hope to continue my involvement for many, many years.

God has blessed my life with a second chance. I will continue to be determined, and with my wonderful family, friends, and new people I meet, I will continuously enjoy the reason why I am still here. I am truly, truly blessed!

"Do not let what you cannot do interfere with what you can do."

—John Wooden

Anna Hoban

ATOU Speaker

I am a very social person and enjoy large gatherings of people. I was born with a disability called Cerebral Palsy, and I use a communication device called a Vanguard to talk. I really enjoy being a speaker for A Touch of Understanding because I love using my device for public speaking and interacting with kids.

Anna Hoban

I love spending time in my community. I enjoy swimming, listening to music, watching my favorite movies (especially *Annie*), and going to aerobics classes at my local gym. I enjoy living in my own apartment with a roommate and my support staff, and I visit my mom and dad on the weekends. I am the co-owner of a business called "Buttons N Bears Oh My!" My business partner, Jackson, designs the buttons and magnets and I make them using a machine. We also sell adorable stuffed animals. I also volunteer at Kaiser once a week. I do the paper-cutting for them.

I am really thankful for A Touch of Understanding. It is very important for children to understand disabilities. Just because someone has a disability, does not mean he or she can't do something; the person just finds another way to do it.

"Genius…means little more than the faculty of perceiving in an un-habitual way."

—William James

Amanda Hussa

ATOU Speaker

My name is Amanda, and I was born with autism. It began when I was a baby. When my mom would breastfeed me she noticed that I was not looking her in the eye. Later on, when I was starting to walk, I would walk on the tips of my toes and often flapped my hands, and she began to think that there was something wrong.

Amanda Hussa

I was starting to talk at one-and-half years old, but then at age two, I stopped learning new words, and slowly started to lose what words I had been saying. I often spoke in what my parents say was "gibberish." My parents said I would try to talk and then look at them as if to say, "You don't have any idea what I'm saying." I couldn't tell people how I felt or what I wanted. I was getting frustrated. I was silenced; I felt as if nobody understood me.

Can you imagine if you couldn't tell someone about being afraid of something? I would have temper tantrums when I couldn't get my needs met. I would panic when I was in crowds or if I heard loud noises. I often held my ears and screamed. Sometimes I would just run away from loud noises and not pay attention to my safety. If I walked past someone starting their car, I would act as if a bomb went off next to me.

My sense of taste was strong. I mostly wanted to eat bland foods like white bread, chicken, mashed potatoes, milk, and cereal or crunchy foods like carrots. Over the years my parents introduced me to salads and other vegetables. They encouraged me to try different foods. I now eat foods such as broccoli, tomatoes, Brussels sprouts, oranges, onions, and garlic that I used to find too strong to eat. I still have trouble eating asparagus and hot peppers.

My skin is very sensitive to touch. When I was in elementary school, I could not wear blue jeans. They felt too rough on my skin. I gradually got used to them. I used to get startled when people tapped me on the shoulder, but I've gotten used to it. I didn't always like to be hugged when I was little, but now I really like hugs.

Autism was not well understood when I was a little girl, and my mom was told that I would be a late talker. I was diagnosed with autism at age four, and my parents started to look for ways to get me to talk. They found an intensive therapy program, and the therapists came to our house and worked with me. I worked with two tutors for six hours a day with only a lunch break.

Within six months, I was talking like most kids my age, so the diligence paid off.

Once I learned how to talk, I had to learn how to play with toys. An occupational therapist taught me how to ride a tricycle and how to blow bubbles. I went through years of therapy to learn how to be around people, and how to play with other kids and cope with noise levels. It was up to my parents to keep me busy with other kids. I took ballet, swimming, and acting classes.

But there was a problem when I started to talk: I talked only about Disney movies, and the movie I liked at the time was *The Lion King*. It would drive my friends and family crazy when I would go on and on about the characters and story. I would always want to talk about Disney cartoons or movies. When someone changed the subject, I would interrupt them and start talking about Disney again. This got really old to other people and they would walk away and avoid talking to me, because they would like to talk about other things.

I have some big problems because of having autism. I have trouble concentrating when I'm trying to do schoolwork. I have learning disabilities, especially in math. One of the biggest challenges I have to deal with is my super-sensitive ears. In the third grade, my doctor recommended getting custom-made earplugs for my ears, because I was so sensitive to noises. I also got some noise-canceling headphones, which were originally made to drown out noise on airplanes. I use them when I go to the movie theater or a rock concert.

I have been bullied a couple of times, when I was in elementary school and when I was in high school. I had great friends who defended me when I was bullied by the sixth graders. The smallest girl in my fourth grade class helped protect me from the bullies, and I am so glad that I knew her.

When I was in high school, I was bullied by a teacher's aide who was supposed to help me in my classes, but said things like, "You are not good at this and you're not good at that," or "I don't trust you." When I went to my English teacher and told her what was going on, the stories came to light and that aide was removed.

When I was sixteen years old, I was beginning to learn how important it was to help other people. I went to Mississippi with my mom and some other people from my church to help victims of Hurricane Katrina. So many people lost everything in the storm and needed a lot of help. It felt good doing things for other people. We cleared debris from inside and outside of houses, helped put down flooring, and sanded and painted walls. I was a stranger volunteering. No one treated me like I had a disability. It was more about what I could do rather than what I couldn't do. After that experience, I became more self-confident. I became more active in volunteer work. I now help regularly with feeding the homeless. I especially love to work with animals. I graduated high school, went to Sierra College, and did some classes such as drama, English, computers, and I was a part of a program called "Supportive Education."

There are some good things about having autism. I have a great memory for memorizing lines from movies and people's names. I tend to think out of the box. I come up with ideas and solutions that no one else may have thought of. I think in pictures like a famous woman named Temple Grandin, who has autism. She has overcome a lot, and made a successful career as an animal expert, and has a Ph.D. in animal science.

I found A Touch of Understanding when I was volunteering at an animal sanctuary and found out that I was good at public speaking. I also enjoyed being around kids. I started being a guest speaker with ATOU in November 2011. It means a lot to volunteer for A Touch if Understanding because I have made a lot of great friends with and without disabilities. The people with disabilities have taught me that it is OK to talk to them, because they are just regular people who are trying to fit in. I love speaking to the kids at the schools because they are good listeners, and they ask me good questions. I usually ask them if they know someone with autism, and most of them tell me they have a friend or a relative who has autism.

I love to tell them my story, and I enjoy seeing students' reactions because it means that they are learning more about the disability and they are getting good insight from my experience with having autism. But I also like to answer their questions because they are so honest and direct. I like to see the students learn how to use the tools that people with disabilities use every day. It gives them a feeling of what it's like to use a white cane, use a wheelchair, have a prosthetic arm or leg, have learning disabilities, or need to use Braille.

Although I have done a lot of things with my family, I don't do much with groups because it overwhelms me. I feel safe with people from A Touch of Understanding. It makes me feel good about myself to think that I am making a difference in the kids' lives. I like that there is camaraderie among the A Touch of Understanding volunteers. A Touch of Understanding Youth F.O.R.C.E. means a lot to me, because I love to see kids and adults at the events and meetings. I like being around people of all ages, and I love to hear people come up with some fun activities for the group to do. I really look forward to the events, because they are exciting and it makes me happy: to make new friends and to see people have a good time.

A Touch of Understanding Youth F.O.R.C.E. has been significant in my life. I enjoy being around people my own age. I didn't know about the social cues of interacting with people and facial expressions. It was easier for me to be around adults because they tend to be more understanding, and know how to interact with me. Whenever I do Youth F.O.R.C.E. activities, I get to be a kid again, which is fun.

One of the things I like to do is read, especially to read about Greek mythology. Another thing I have enjoyed in the past few years is writing. I can see a story in my head like I'm watching a movie. So, I started putting my stories down on paper. I've completed two short stories. I finished a screenplay about Persephone, a Greek goddess who falls in love with Apollo, the Sun god. I decided to try writing a story as a screenplay because I like stage direction and movies. I hope to someday publish my stories and maybe direct or be in the movies.

While I was speaking at A Touch of Understanding event, I met Rob Stewart from a show on PBS called "Rob on the Road." He was so impressed that he had me in his documentary called "Autism: Emerging from the Maze." After that, I was a part of another TV special called "Bully" on KCRA Channel 3. Last year, I was on the board of speakers at the UC Davis Mind Institute, and there was a segment on autism at their "Minds Behind the MIND" lecture series. I am currently attending a film school that was started by John Travolta's older brother Joey. I am learning about camera work, editing, makeup, costume design, writing, acting, and lighting.

Autism is a part of me, but it does not define me. I still face challenges every day, but I have learned to find the positive in life, and laugh more.

165

"Accept the challenges so you can feel the exhilaration of victory."
—George S. Patton

Denise Berkes Sanchez

ATOU Speaker

Denise Berkes Sanchez

I grew up in the Sacramento area. As a young child, I went to Bowling Green Elementary School where they had a fantastic Orthopedic Handicapped Department with physical therapists, speech therapists, and amazing teachers to help children with all types of physical disabilities.

I was born with my condition. My disability is a combination of several things; I have Scoliosis, Lordosis, and a mild case of Spina Bifida. These are all problems with the spine. Currently my spine is fusing (becoming rigid and immoveable), so now I have what is called Cervicogenic headache and all I can say is ouch! It is not uncommon to have a two-week straight migraine-type headache. I had what was thought to be Arthrogryposis Multiplex Conginita for years, but then it was decided I may actually have Multiple Petrygerium Syndrome. It is really much easier to say. I'm quite short and my joints are stiff and "owie."

To help, I have shoes that are specially made for me. My feet are not shaped normally and one leg is longer than the other so getting a good shoe can mean the difference of walking independently or having to use crutches. (I have a WONDERFUL pedorthist in Auburn, California, who makes my shoes and he is nothing if not magic!) I also use crutches on rare occasions if I have no other options. We all need to get from "point A to point B" whatever way necessary.

I have a wonderful extended family, supportive friends, and a husband who loves me very much. As a teenager, I never thought a guy would want to marry me because I am disabled. Well, that's evidently rubbish! My husband helps me when I need it without ever making me feel like he is going out of his way. I am so happy.

Growing up with a first cousin who has very involved Cerebral Palsy was very beneficial, because we had one another for support and encouragement. Over the years, life has given us differing challenges, but the love and comfort we derive from one another is a priceless gift. It takes a lot of determination to succeed in life, but throw a disability in there and that is a HUGE obstacle that makes you have to find more fortitude and determination hidden in places you never thought to look.

I found out about ATOU when I was in my thirties, and knew it was an organization I wanted to be a part of. If ATOU had been around when I was young, I think things may have run a bit smoother for me in school but alas it was not, and I suffered though countless acts of bullying and unnecessary emotional hardship. ATOU gives speakers the opportunity to share their stories and touch the lives of kids in the effort to prevent both disabled kids from being bullied and potential bullies from acting out. ATOU is really a wonderful organization that is making the world a better place, one school at a time.

I spent time at Sacramento City College and American River College. Both campuses had fantastic disability resource centers. I eventually went to CSU Sacramento to earn my bachelor's degree in psychology. I knew I wanted to help families (as well as individuals), and focus on disabilities within the family. The person with the disability has challenges, but so does the whole family. The family isn't the problem, the problem is the problem. I went to graduate school and received a Master's Degree in Marriage and Family Therapy, so currently I'm a Psychotherapist working on obtaining licensure.

"I know of no more encouraging fact than the unquestionable ability of man to elevate his life by a conscious endeavor."

—*Henry David Thoreau*

Matt Cardoza

ATOU Speaker

Matt Cardoza

In 2012, I began going to a stroke support group at American River College. In this group, I met people who had gone through just what I had gone through. I met women and men who were older and younger than me. I remain very close to members of this group today, and I can say that I love every one of them. Doris Hernandez-Morales (see page 155) is the founder, and she is very dedicated to the stroke group to which I belong (for more information on this group you can email: doris_ hernandezmorales@yahoo.com). Through both Doris and Paula Henry (another friend and member of the group, see page 154), I was introduced to A Touch of Understanding (ATOU). I attended my first ATOU presentation as a spectator in December of 2013 in Rancho Cordova.

I could see first-hand how this program touches the lives of everyone involved in both the speaker portion and in the activities. During the presentation, children participate in several hands-on activities and ask questions. During the presentation, I was inspired so much that I wanted to start volunteering the next day.

I got live-scanned and submitted my paperwork to ATOU. Within a couple of weeks, I created my video and gave my first speech on August, 27, 2014. I try to teach students a little about stroke, tell them my story and, most importantly, let them know to never give up on their dreams. ATOU is a great program, and its volunteers touch the lives of others.

"Two roads diverged in a wood, and I—I took the one less traveled by, and that has made all the difference."

—Robert Frost

Erik Greenan

ATOU Speaker

I have cerebral palsy, due to being born two months early, and I spent the first three weeks of my life in the hospital. Cerebral palsy is a condition that prevents my arms and legs from fully functioning. I could not get around until my parents got me a "Crawligator" when I was one. A Crawligator is a green plastic gator on wheels that I could lay on and pull myself around. My mother went crazy with me pulling everything out of the drawers in the kitchen.

In my second year, I finally rolled over. What a celebration when I did that! I also got my first pair of glasses because I am

Erik Greenan

very farsighted. My glasses opened up a whole new world for me. I became interested in things on the shelves in the grocery store, much to my mom's chagrin. I did not talk until I was four years old. Interestingly, I never spoke baby talk; the first words out of my mouth were full sentences. Now my family calls me "motor mouth." (I guess I am making up for lost time.)

I've had several surgeries on my legs to loosen them up, because they can get very tight. I will never walk or run, but I can sure get around in my wheelchair. My parents sometimes threaten to take away my driver's license when I go too fast in the chair or "pop wheelies." When I was younger, I participated in Special Olympics, and have lots of medals hanging on my wall.

I love being in the water. I took survival lessons in the water when I was a baby. Just put a life jacket on me and I'm good to go! I spent my childhood years boating with my family. One of my first experiences was riding on my dad's shoulders as he stood on a wooden disc being slowly pulled by our boat. I graduated to riding in a tube behind the boat. I recently got to participate in water sports with Disabled Sports at Donner Lake. I got to jet-ski, tube, kayak, and sail. I had a blast, and they even had time for my mom and dad to try the jet-ski.

I like to work out three days a week at Planet Fitness. I do weights and the treadmill. I can stand and walk on the treadmill, as long as I hold onto the bars. Once in a while, I use a walker for strengthening, but I cannot walk for very long.

I have worked at Century Theater in Roseville, California, for almost sixteen years. I like being there, and the perks are great. My family is spoiled with free movies, popcorn, and drinks. Sundays are usually my family's movie day. I recently started another job with Country Waffles. I do sign waving for them on Tuesday mornings. I also keep busy doing volunteer work at food banks, and I clean and play with the rabbits at Petco.

I'm also a gamer. I love PS4 and am relentless to finish levels. I like a lot of old television shows and have a lot of them on CD. I'm still learning how to use Dragon Speak on the computer. Dragon Speak is a talking program that interprets my words and writes them down for me. The program can do a lot of crazy things and types words I do not say. It is still learning my voice.

I really enjoy volunteering with ATOU. I even got a president's award for volunteering. I am proud and happy to be a part of ATOU's family that respects and loves me for who I am.

Written by Erik, with help from his mother, Judi.

"We must let go of the life we have planned, so as to accept the one that is waiting for us."

—Joseph Campbell

Mary L. Herdegen
ATOU Speaker

It was the Friday afternoon before Memorial Day weekend, 2010. I wasn't working that day and decided to enjoy a walk in my neighborhood on the beautiful, sunny day. As I left the house, I told my husband, Dave, that I'd be back in an hour. However, my life as I knew it, changed forever fifteen minutes

Mary L. Herdegen

into my walk. It would be nearly five months before I returned to my home and family.

I was struck, head-on by a car travelling more than 40 mph. Unfortunately, because I had no identification or cell phone with me, I was classified as "Jane Doe" for nearly six hours. With the assistance of the Placer County Sheriff's Department, my family identified me at Sutter Roseville Hospital. My husband was told by the trauma doctors that I was critically injured, with multiple broken bones, and a severe traumatic brain injury (TBI). It was questionable whether I would make it through the night, as the pressure in my skull was increasing due to my brain swelling.

At Sutter Roseville Hospital, I was in a coma for two weeks and had several surgeries in an effort to "Humpty-Dumpty" me back together again. At times, due to my fragile condition, the doctors had to forgo continued orthopedic surgeries. I don't remember those early days of recovery.

In July 2010, I was transferred from Sutter Roseville Hospital to California Pacific Medical Center (CPMC) in San Francisco. It would serve as my 'home by the bay' for the next four months. It was a painful and difficult time for me, away from my family and friends in Granite Bay. The days were grueling for me, and my nights were lonely. My days were filled with endless hours of therapy (physical, speech, occupational, recreational) and ongoing medical procedures, all in an effort to send me home to my family, who I desperately missed. While at CPMC, I was absent from several family milestones; including my son's twenty-first birthday, and my twenty ninth wedding anniversary.

Despite the medical challenges I was facing on a daily basis while hospitalized at CPMC, we were provided with tremendous support from family, friends, neighbors, and coworkers. One family friend established a website and provided email updates to those concerned about me. Folks were also encouraged to communicate with me, via cards and letters, while I was in the hospital for several months. The communiques cheered me, and helped me still feel connected to home, despite the distance.

I must say, my husband and kids ate much better than I did, during the early months I was hospitalized. Two of our neighbors developed a sign-up sheet for volunteers to prepare home-cooked dinners, and deliver them to our home. It was quite a system: with an ice chest conveniently located on the porch for meal drop-offs. Still others provided my family with food gift cards, walked our dogs, and assisted with other family chores.

By mid-October 2010, my family brought me home to continue my recovery. For the next eighteen months, I attended therapy three times a week and endured additional orthopedic surgeries, in my quest to try to regain all that I had lost, both physically and cognitively. I had to relearn how to do everything. I needed assistance to do most daily activities, including toileting, showering/grooming, dressing myself, and meal preparation. It was almost a year before I was able to walk independently again.

During this time, my husband, daughter and son, were trying to resume their lives, "pre-accident," while also having to take care of me. My husband worked as a procurement manager for Hewlett Packard in Roseville, where he subsequently retired, after twenty-five years, in February 2014. Our daughter, Shannon, was working as (and still is) a community services officer with the Placer County Sheriff's Department, and our son, Derek, was in his second year at Sierra Community

College. Shannon moved home with us for a year, burning every hour of her accrued vacation and sick leave to assist in my care. For Derek, the stress of my accident caused him to come down with mononucleosis, and he struggled to fully resume his college curriculum for the next two years. In December 2014, following in his sister's footsteps, our son earned his B.S. degree in criminal justice.

This accident sideswiped my family. It was also during this time that my ninety-one year old father, who was suffering from Alzheimer's disease, passed away. About a year before my accident, my family had moved dad into a care facility about two miles from my home. I worked as a senior management analyst for Placer County, coordinating its Federal and State Government Affairs Programs for over fifteen years. When I wasn't working, I would enthusiastically visit dad several times a week, bringing him special treats and playing games with him to help maintain as much of his memory as possible. We both looked forward to our time together. After my accident, I did not see my father again for six months. Sadly, he passed away, five months after I came home from CPMC.

My severe traumatic brain injury prevented me from returning to my job at Placer County. My nearly twenty-year career was cut short, through no fault of my own. At times, it has been one of the most difficult accident outcomes for me.

By October 2014, I realized that physically, I was about as good as I was going to get, and I finally found the courage to attend a monthly TBI Support Group at Sutter Roseville. Today, I continue to live with pain, headaches, memory and cognitive deficiencies, nerve damage, vision problems, depression, anxiety, and insomnia. I was extremely self-conscious about

174

my traumatic brain injury. Friends would say to me: "But, you look so normal." Or, in an effort to make me feel better: "I can't remember things either...it's our age."

I first learned about ATOU from the Sutter TBI Support Group in the summer of 2015. At that time, I was ready to find volunteer opportunities to share my experience of surviving a near-death trauma, and living with a TBI. After further researching ATOU, visiting their Granite Bay Office in September 2015, and meeting ATOU Founder Leslie DeDora, I felt like Goldilocks. I had found just the right volunteer "fit" for me.

I started as a volunteer speaker in October 2015. I consider myself an ATOU "newbie," compared to the tenure of most ATOU volunteers. From the beginning, ATOU's dedicated staff and volunteers have made me feel welcome and comfortable. ATOU provides a tremendous service to the students it serves by teaching them to show kindness, patience, and understanding to those with disabilities. And for its volunteers, it provides us with an atmosphere of warmth, caring, support, and gratitude. Ironically, ATOU has helped me become more accepting and comfortable of my disability. For that, I am eternally grateful.

"Keep your face to the sunshine and you cannot see a shadow."
—Helen Keller

Dwight Lunkley

ATOU Speaker

Over the years of running on this complicated and challenging course that we call life, with its tight and twisting tedious sections, rough and bumpy sections, smooth high speed sections, and holes, ditches, and washes that seem to leap out of nowhere in

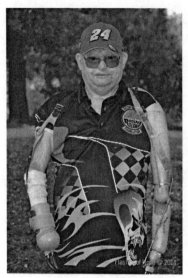

Dwight Lunkley

an effort to knock you off-course, I have learned one invaluable lesson. It is summed up in three principles that have become my motto and drive every aspect of my life. Never Give Up, Never Give In, and Never Quit!

Keep these three principles in mind as I recount to you the most significant event in my life. It has tested my resolve on those fundamental principles beyond any limits I could have ever possibly imagined. The day-to-day reality of that very trial has impacted every aspect of my life, redefined for me the boundaries of what is possible and impossible, and defined for me the struggle to survive, recover, and regain my life. Even now, after all this time, as I daily continue to push the boundaries of my capabilities outward, giving up, giving in, or quitting would spell an end to the growing, vibrant, exciting, and rewarding life that has now become mine to live.

Change comes to everyone, but not normally as abruptly as it did for me and my very good friend, Bill Rigsby. On July 29, 1994, in the blistering sun of a remote area of the Nevada desert, life as I knew it literally went up in smoke. The off-road desert buggy in which we were riding on the Fallon 250 desert racecourse hit a wash, flipped end over end, burst into flames, and slid to a stop, coming to rest on its right side. It continued burning, the flames being fed by leaking fuel. Bill's harness burned through and he was able to crawl free, still on fire and burning. I was unable to release my harness and was trapped in

176

the blazing buggy until help arrived a few minutes or more later.

I was pulled from the vehicle by fellow racer who extinguished the flames and gingerly cut the harness to get me free. I was barely alive, on the edge of conscious and deeply burned over nearly the entire surface of my body. Although I was burned extensively, I felt no pain. That may have been due to shock or because the burns penetrated so deep that all the nerve endings were gone. At that point, I felt certain my life was at its end. My life's energy was draining quickly from me and I could feel death knocking at the door. I was amazingly calm.

Although I could not see, I asked the person tending to me to watch out for my kids who were in the main pit area. I prayed, "Well, Lord, I pushed myself all the way on this one. I can't do anything for myself and it doesn't appear there is much anyone else can do. It's your call, if I live or die. I will be happy with whatever you decide." It was my hope that God would allow me to be around to see my kids finish growing up, but at that point, it didn't seem too likely.

At that point, I resolved myself to lie still, wait to see which way the pendulum would swing, and let all those who had gathered do whatever they could do to help. It was my hope that God would allow me to be around to see my kids finish growing up, but at that point, it didn't seem too likely. My mind was absorbing all the sounds and voices that were around me. From all that, and how I felt, I gathered a good sense for the situation and had a clear understanding of how grave things were. I locked myself in a struggle to just try and stay alive and was holding with all the physical and mental strength that I had left to hold onto that very thin slip of thread that was now my only link to this world.

Although the accident was remote, a squad of U.S. Marines who were flagged down on Highway 50 showed up on the scene to help. Everyone who was there, mostly other racers, helped however they could. The grave nature of our burn injuries were way beyond the experience of anyone there. The collective effort was to do the best they could do to keep us alive long enough to get us evacuated to get adequate medical care. The Marines called in a U.S. Navy helicopter, and Bill and I were flown to the Washoe Medical Center in Reno, Nevada. We arrived there one hour and forty-five minutes after the burns.

The trauma room doctors at Washoe worked feverishly to stabilize both Bill and myself in an effort to save our lives. We both coded more than once in the ER. It was apparent to them that our needs far-exceeded their capabilities, and that if we were to have any chance of surviving our massive burn injuries, both of us needed to be in the care of a specialized burn center.

After performing some surgical procedures on us both for the burns, a respirator to help my lungs function, and cardiac care for Bill, the Washoe trauma doctors made the necessary arrangements and the two of us were airlifted separately to the UC Davis Regional Burn Center in Sacramento.

Despite the valiant efforts of the Burn Team, Bill died twelve days later. I lingered near death in a coma for nearly seven weeks on a ventilator to help me breath, and a feeding tube to pump nourishment into my stomach. The best odds given to my family regarding my survival chances were 1 percent, and the director of the Burn Center, Dr. Missavage, stated flatly, "I am being extremely liberal at that. Your brother is in serious trouble."

I received grafting on over two-thirds of my body's surface, had my left arm amputated nearly to the shoulder, my right hand amputated through the wrist, suffered massive muscle loss and tissue damage, and had my face reconstructed. My nose was gone but they would deal with that later; keeping me alive carried a much higher priority.

Although the total losses were staggering, to everyone's surprise, I responded extremely well to treatment and after just over two months, I recovered enough to be transferred to the UC Davis Medical Center's Rehabilitation Unit. I was terribly weak and had lost over 40 pounds. Despite the expectations of the rehab physicians that I would never be able to function normally, care for myself, or even return home, ten months after the fiery crash, I returned home to reestablish life with my son and daughter. Just fifteen months after that fateful day, I returned to work with my employer of eighteen years. Only twenty-three months after the accident, I was once again harnessed into the seat of an off-road race vehicle (an awesome class-8 Chevy truck) and was blasting over unforgiving desert terrain. Who says the impossible isn't possible?

Over twenty-one years have elapsed since that pivotal moment for me in Nevada's high desert, and here I am, able to share my story with others. No one can tell me that miracles don't happen or that the impossible isn't possible. I have had an incredible journey of over twenty-one years that began at death's door. For someone who wasn't supposed to survive, function normally, rise to his feet without assistance, feed himself, or ever be able to return home, to still be here is so profound that it makes being alive each day exciting and worth all the trials along the way.

Yes, I have traveled far. All that effort, all the battles and struggles to overcome the obstacles were well-worth the cost to have the privilege to live the exciting, rewarding, and meaningful life that God has granted me in the aftermath of that life-altering event. The simple truth is there is life after a traumatic debilitating illness or injury, and that life can extend far beyond the ordinary into the extraordinary.

Two years ago, my incredible journey led me to ATOU. ATOU encourages acceptance and respect for all individuals, promoting understanding and empathy. Each individual learns first-hand from disabled volunteers what their disabilities are, how they became disabled, how they overcome those disabilities, as well as tools used to adapt to everyday life and live as good a lifestyle as possible. The hands-on portion of the workshops gives everyone the opportunity to use adaptive devices and briefly walk in the shoes of those with disabilities.

I became involved with ATOU at the urgings of my cousin Susie Glover*, who was one of those supporting me from the day of my burn injuries to the present. Even though I dragged my feet for a long time, I am truly grateful that she never gave up on me to become involved with ATOU. ATOU's purpose goes far beyond its mission to educate and promote understanding for disabled people. It also provides a tremendous life lesson about facing and overcoming adversity. I am sure this message comes through in the examples set by the volunteer speakers and all of the dedicated staff members and volunteers who work to enlighten others. Despite any differences we have, every individual matters and has value, and we should treat everyone with kindness and respect.

My involvement with ATOU has not only broadened my horizons and afforded me the opportunity to share my story, but it has allowed me to develop friendships with the remarkable

*Susie Glover, see page 135

and inspirational staff and volunteers who make up the ATOU family. Life is indeed an exciting and rewarding experience if one always moves forward. I will forever be grateful that the course of my own destiny has brought me to ATOU, and has given me the opportunity to be a part of such a noble and worthy cause. It just doesn't get any better than that! Any obstacle can be overcome, and a rich and rewarding life can be obtained. Life is indeed good!

"Where there is great love, there are always miracles."

—*Willa Cather*

Jill C. Mason

ATOU Speaker who conceived the idea of *Voices of a Dream*

I got a whole bushel of lemons when I was twenty-six, and the only choice I saw was to make lemonade. That is how I was raised, anyway, to make the most out of what I had and to see the glass half full. This is why my reaction to my life changing so drastically has been smoother. And, it is this mentality that attracts me to ATOU—being around folks who also choose to make lemonade.

I was a triathlete, runner, and marketing professional in Silicon Valley. I graduated from Santa Clara University in 1999, with a major in English. Following my desire to use writing in my job, I joined the engineering firm Lowney Associates

Jill C. Mason

as the Marketing Communications Specialist. I managed the website, the monthly postcard production, and quarterly newsletter we mailed to a targeted list of clients, in addition to the public relations and internal company events. Lowney paid for my 2003 master's degree in mass communications from San Jose State University.

In 2003, I joined Mountain View Master's swim team for my triathlon training. Triathlons are one race of swimming, biking, and running. The head coach of Mountain View Master's Swim Team, Alan, was a graduate of MIT in Boston. He had his master's degree from Stanford University and worked as a mechanical engineer at Applied Materials in Sunnyvale. He had six U.S. Patents for his engineering work. After two months on his swim team, he asked me out. I was dumbfounded and I, of course, said "yes!"

Alan and I trained for triathlons, took weekend trips, went out to eat, and went to sporting events. We often rode our bikes together in the Silicon Valley. Mornings were for swimming, and evenings often involved a training run and going to dinner. On April 11, 2004, we took a morning bike ride before Easter brunch with his mom in Santa Rosa.

We were hit on our bicycles from behind by a sixty-nine-year-old drunk driver with a blood alcohol content of .34, and the fairy-tale was over. Alan was killed instantly and I, riding in front of Alan, was thrown off my bike by the 55 mph hit. The first responders said the helmet saved my life (which is an important fact I tell the students in ATOU workshops). I was taken to Santa Rosa Memorial Hospital and kept on life support for at least a week. My spinal cord was severed at thoracic 12, and I had a traumatic brain injury, which required a peritoneal shunt to drain fluid off my swollen brain.

I was transferred to Santa Clara Valley Medical Center after a month, which is where I had physical, occupational, and speech therapies, once I emerged from my two-month-long coma. Some of my close friends started a website for me (www.jillmason.com) on April 14, 2004, just three days after being hit. My brother managed it for at least a year, and I updated it for a few years after that when my brain was healed enough to handle it.

After five months, I was discharged from Santa Clara Valley Medical Center, not to my upstairs apartment in Mountain View, but to my parents' home in Grass Valley, where I grew up. Family and friends modified many parts of the house prior to my discharge, for which I am forever grateful. Following two years of speech, physical, and occupational therapies in Grass Valley, I (once again) moved out of my parents' house to Sacramento, California. Luckily, I found an apartment complex just being constructed, so the workers made modifications to meet my specific needs. I did all three therapies again at UC Davis Medical Center in Sacramento.

Wanting to share my story and put my master's degree to good use (since it was only a few years old), I developed a digital presentation to give to schools about the dangers of drinking and driving, and have been presenting to schools since 2006. These presentations often are associated with the Every 15 Minutes or Red Ribbon Week programs that high schools and grammar schools use to influence smart decisions.

After six months of driving-with-my-hands lessons in 2007, two written DMV tests, and a behind the wheel driving test, I regained my driver's license and bought a sedan. In 2008, I bought my home in Sacramento after a lengthy search. My realtor's contractor husband modified parts of my house; I moved in, and restarted my life. I wrote a book with my aunt's (very patient and professional) editorial help. Writing with a head injury is not an easy game (and neither is editing a brain-injured author). My book chronicles the accident, a bit before, but mostly after. The book is used by resident doctors at UC Davis Medical Center to gain a better understanding of traumatic brain injury and spinal cord injury.

I received a recommendation to my website to enter an essay contest to carry the Olympic Torch in April 2008 when it came to San Francisco. The selection committee chose my essay, with about 30 others, in addition to corporate sponsor representatives, so I carried the torch in the (luckily flat) Marina District of the city.

I raise money for non-profit organizations annually at a swim meet Alan's Mountain View Master's team hosts in his honor. And, prior to non-profits being the benefactors of Mountain View Masters, I used the money raised by Mountain View Masters to buy two digital pace clocks for Alan's high school swim team.

I found ATOU from a response to a Facebook post about my wish to volunteer for SOMETHING. The group's goal of encouraging children to be kind to all, especially folks with disabilities, mirrors my mentality. ATOU has helped me to show folks that a wheelchair is just a piece of equipment I use to get around, it does not define who I am. The folks with ATOU are extraordinarily patient and accepting. It's this mentality that draws me to this group.

They are what they teach: they are patient, kind, and understanding. And it is this way of being that is what ATOU teaches Northern California students. Everyone can find a similarity with stories shared by ATOU speakers. There's a reason why this happened to me, maybe it was to help ATOU educate the future of the world about treating others well, regardless of their disabilities.

*Jill Mason's book, *Couldn't Happen to Me*, is available on Amazon.

"We should all be concerned about the future because we will have to spend the rest of our lives there."

—*Charles Franklin Kettering*

Sandy Puleo

ATOU Speaker

Sandy Puleo

When I was born, the doctors told my parents, "Your son will never walk." I was born with spina bifida, a birth defect that affects everyone who has it differently. I have no working nerves below my knees; as a result, I can't feel anything below my knees and nothing in that part of my body works; everything above the knees works just fine.

My parents set up two long bars in my yard. They encouraged me to walk between the bars using my hands to hold me up. I did that for nearly two years. My parents were right and the doctors were wrong. I got my upper legs so strong I could walk, with the help of a cane, and no longer needed the bars.

In spite of my strength, I walked with a limp and, as a result, was a very self-conscious kid. I wanted very much to be "normal" like the other kids. I had a fourth grade teacher I liked and trusted a lot. I shared my feelings with her. I told her that "I felt I was a disability." Her response was: "You are not a disability; you're a child like everyone else, who happens to have a disability." Until that talk, I could never separate me being a disability from me having a disability.

My fourth grade teacher changed my life forever. Almost instantly I had self-esteem, something I had never experienced. It was very cool. I was a good and competitive student. Academics were the only place I felt equally skilled as the other kids. My self-esteem increased so much I decided to run for student body president of my junior high school. I was elected and re-elected, not because kids felt sorry for me, but because they knew I would be good at it, and I was!

I have always had a passion for sports. When I was a kid, more than five decades ago, I was unable to physically participate in most sports, so I decided to do the next best thing: I became a sports writer and sports statistician. I did this from junior high through college at California State University, Sacramento (CSUS). I was even hired as a part-time sports writer by my local newspaper, the *Vallejo Times Herald*, and then by *The Sacramento Bee*. I received a B.A. degree in government/ journalism from CSUS, and then received an internship working for a congressman in Washington, D.C. It was interesting and lots of fun living and working near the pulse of our government.

I have never let my disability stop me from doing much of anything in my life. My family and friends will attest to that. I have spent a lifetime doing things people didn't think I could do. Early on, it was fun showing people I could do things they thought should be impossible for me to do. Now I just do them for me. I have nothing left to prove to anyone.

I try to live my life to the fullest, and have had fun doing things like skydiving, parasailing, driving my car and a boat, water and snow skiing, swimming and scuba diving, rock climbing, and swimming with dolphins. My life revolves around my wife, Rhonda, two stepsons, an adopted son and daughter, four grandchildren, and more than five dozen foster children, who live or have lived with us over the last seventeen years.

My first experience with ATOU was over three years ago, when a friend told me it was a place I would enjoy. He was right; I really enjoy it. I don't just enjoy ATOU; it is a place I NEED to be. When I am involved with ATOU, no matter where we are, there is never, ever a judgmental voice in the room. It is always a comfortable and fun environment for me. When we go to schools, if I can stop one child from being teased or bullied, it makes my day. We accomplish that goal at every school, which is why I am still involved—and I will be as long as possible. Everyone in ATOU, including me, is there to make a positive difference in the lives of the people we encounter. We do that every day.

"We know what we are, but know not what we may be."
—William Shakespeare

Chris Roe

ATOU Speaker

I have lived in Sacramento, California my whole life. I was born with a condition called Arthrogryposis, which means my muscles and joints are not fully developed, so I have used adaptive equipment throughout my life. I used a walker and leg braces until age five,

Chris Roe

187

and then I used arm crutches until age fifteen. Now, since my back surgery when I was fifteen, I use a wheelchair full time because it's easier to get around.

I completed high school and then graduated with an associate degree in computer science. My decision to use the wheelchair full time made it easier to carry all of my belongings safely to school.

I was blessed with the ability to be able to drive a car, and have been since the age of seventeen. My car is fully equipped with hand controls, and has a ramp so I can have my wheelchair on the passenger side. Being able to drive gives me the ability to get around on my own.

When I was twenty-seven, I met the amazing group named A Touch of Understanding. This has been a great journey, and it's just getting started. I think every school need to see this program in every grade level, because it is that important. From the speakers, to the workshops, and all of the volunteers involved, I think it really shows the kids how to relate to others in daily life activities. It is an honor to be involved in such a valuable and worthwhile cause to help give back to the next generation with the right education to live their lives.

I make the best out of every situation, and I like to spread positive cheer. I know that we all want to be happy and enjoy life, so live your life to the fullest and enjoy every day you are given!

"When you come to a fork in the road, take it."

—*Yogi Berra*

Duane Wyatt

ATOU Speaker

Duane Wyatt

I was diagnosed with Autism Spectrum Disorder, specifically Asperger's Syndrome by Dr. Denali Tice, a psychiatrist at UC Davis Medical Center. The diagnosis was made in 2015. My twin brother, Dean, did not exhibit signs of Autism Spectrum Disorder. He was much more outgoing than I was, and he was a first-team basketball player. I seldom talked, made few friends, and was happiest by myself. I remember taking an IQ test because my parents were concerned. I believe they self-diagnosed my quietness as shyness.

I still remember my basketball coach asking me in the locker room after a practice why I never looked at anyone. I did not know the answer to his question. I was not coordinated and gave competitive basketball a good try, but finally, I quit the team because I seldom played in games. Dean and I looked alike and we were teased occasionally—people called us "twin" instead of our names when they wanted one of us to come over and talk.

I was raised on a farm, and our chores included feeding the livestock and horses daily. I had orphan lambs that I liked to feed and raise—they often became my inseparable friends. I was much more comfortable around my animal friends than my human ones.

My parents did not understand my psyche. They forced me to go to Methodist youth fellowship and other social events, when I really just wanted to stay home.

When I was thirteen, and in 4-H, I was exhibiting my lamb at the local county fair when I heard sounds coming from under the grandstand. I was intrigued, so I investigated and spent much time at the amateur radio station I found there. I was intrigued by the Morse code. Morse is loads of fun, challenging, non-threatening to me, and wholesome. It is a fun way to make friends without having to leave one's home or look at the new friend. It is stress-diverting, and I became a Morse code expert.

One year ago, I attended (under duress) my wife's family reunion. I found a recliner in the corner of the living room and tried to escape the situation. I closed my eyes and imagined being at home, where there weren't all of the people. My mother-in-law came up to me and asked me why I did not talk and socialize with people. I did go to the patio and made an effort to talk, but became angry and shouted at everyone to hurry up and take the family photo, and that I was going to walk the fifteen or so miles home. My wife came after me in the car and took me home. I was so stressed out and acted unpredictably. It was so embarrassing for me, my wife, and my children.

I assembled an amateur radio-Morse code exhibit that I present at local events. At the last ScholarShare event at Fairytale Town in Sacramento, a teenager came to the display. He was fascinated by the Morse code demonstration I was giving. He had difficulty talking because he stuttered. He finally found something that was impressive to see, fun to do, and something he could do that his friends could not do. He came to my exhibit four times that day.

I contacted a speech therapist in Granite Bay, telling her about the teen with the speech issue. She referred me to the fine people at A Touch of Understanding. A dialogue was started and I told staff at ATOU about my Autism Spectrum Disorder issue. I have been telling my life story ever since. For some reason (I think that my prayers to God help me), I am usually not nervous to talk about my life in front of the students. It amazes me and my family. However, I cannot look directly at the audience and someone else typically calls on the students who have questions. I also show the ATOU Morse code poster and explain that Morse was first thought about by Samuel Morse in 1832 while on a seagoing voyage.

I show the three Morse instruments and explain that Morse was used by spies behind enemy lines in the world wars to seek rescue. It also was used extensively by Abraham Lincoln to message his Union Army generals in the civil war. Recruits who were too young to become Union Army soldiers sometimes became President Lincoln's telegraphers. Special Forces officers learn Morse code—they can signal for help by using sound (whistling) or light (flashlights). The periscopes in modern submarines have a light that can be used to send Morse code, if needed.

In addition, the CIA trains modern spies in Morse code. On the grounds of the CIA are granite and copper sculptures that are part of the "Kryptos" sculpture. There are Morse code inscriptions on these granite sculptures. The Kryptos sculpture has never been fully decoded, with final inscriptions eluding modern government cryptographers and other code breakers.

"A single act of kindness throws out roots in all directions, and the roots spring up and make new trees."

—*Amelia Earhart*

Matson Sewell

ATOU Supporter, Arata Brothers Trustee

Matson Sewell

As a parent and a trustee of a funding organization, I have never seen a unique offering like A Touch of Understanding, and I have a very personal reason for wanting to see ATOU in as many schools as possible. I have two sons who, when they were in grade school, shared a list of diagnoses that included ADD, ADHD, OCD, Oppositional Defiance Disorder, and rule-out Asperger's Syndrome. They had the "invisible disabilities" that ATOU workshops cover in their training to enhance empathic intelligence.

One son in particular developed into a powder keg. What I did not know for a number of months was that a group of kids in my son's classroom had psyched out the strategy to covertly push him into a meltdown. You'd think once the problem was identified, it could be resolved. It could not. Ultimately, each teacher declared that he or she could only respond to the problem behavior—that was my son's—and couldn't monitor the covert operations contributing to his meltdowns. So from the third to eighth grades there was no resolution to the problem, other than my son growing a tougher hide and learning strategies to remove himself from provocation.

I have no doubt that an ATOU workshop in his fourth-grade class would have helped tremendously, because this kind of

192

covert meanness—the intoxicating power of provoking another person into acting out and getting in trouble—could not continue under the bright light and open discussion of choosing kindness. I saw some of those classmates looking sideways at my son as I had to remove him from the school. Their expressions were often more than a little worried... Did I go too far? Did I cause serious harm? And the truth was, they had. We survived a few very frightening years in which my son believed there was no place in the world he belonged once he left home. Twice he attempted serious self-harm.

I don't consider my sons the victims and the other kids perpetrators. They were all victims of the inability for ordinary school administrative processes to address covert bullying. Long after the worst of it, a former classmate approached my son at a reunion and apologized for his behavior of fifteen years earlier. It had bothered him ever since. I'm happy to report that my sons are now well-adjusted young adults. But for both, public school was often an unnecessarily painful, daily lesson in social failure.

ATOU enhances empathic intelligence by starting with the most visible, tangible disabilities, moving onto invisible disabilities and ultimately moving onto self-acceptance in the ways all of us need to accept what we think should be hidden from others. It is a remarkably effective and powerful program delivered with extraordinary grace. There are so few experiences our kids can have in schools that enhance their empathic intelligence in ways so profound and so lasting.

Epilogue

You have heard many of the voices of A Touch of Understanding through the pages of this book, which is a tribute to ATOU and the folks who are part of the team – the ATOU Family. There are other voices of ATOU you have not heard, some of whom have passed away since we started many years ago. We are grateful to everyone who has played a role in the development, growth, and expansion of ATOU. There will be many new voices to hear as we continue, with more generous individuals willing to share their stories, their dreams, their challenges and their victories, eager to enlighten the minds of schoolchildren and adults.

I thank God for the dream of A Touch of Understanding, for the priceless gift of working with my father and the incredible ATOU team members, past and present. We are on an exciting journey, starting with the early years when it was just my father and me providing the workshops. Now, in 2016, our team members share this mission with more than a thousand students every month. I am thankful to each member of our ATOU Family, our volunteers, our staff, our Board of Directors and of course, our donors, all of whom are essential to ATOU.

Thoughtful planning is going into expanding the reach of our programs. We invite you to join us on this incredible ATOU journey. It is sure to be an enriching experience for everyone involved now and for generations to come.

Thank you!

—Leslie DeDora, Co-founder and Executive Director
www.touchofunderstanding.org

Index

CPSIA information can be obtained
at www.ICGtesting.com
Printed in the USA
FSOW02n0348110716
22429FS